JARGON 55

BY JAMES BROUGHTON

*Books*

THE PLAYGROUND 1949

THE BALLAD OF MAD JENNY 1949

MUSICAL CHAIRS 1950

AN ALMANAC FOR AMORISTS 1955

TRUE & FALSE UNICORN 1957

THE RIGHT PLAYMATE 1964

THE WATER CIRCLE 1965

TIDINGS 1965

LOOK IN LOOK OUT 1968

HIGH KUKUS 1969

*Films*

MOTHER'S DAY 1948

ADVENTURES OF JIMMY 1950

FOUR IN THE AFTERNOON 1951

LOONY TOM 1951

THE PLEASURE GARDEN 1953

THE BED 1968

NUPTIAE 1969

THE GOLDEN POSITIONS 1970

JAMES BROUGHTON

COLLECTED POEMS 1949-1969

# *A LONG UNDRESSING*

*They say death's a going to bed; I doubt it;*
*but anyhow life's a long undressing.*
—WALTER DE LA MARE

THE JARGON SOCIETY: NEW YORK: 1971

ACKNOWLEDGEMENTS
Certain of these poems first appeared in the following publications.

MAGAZINES: *Botteghe Oscure, Poetry, Folder, Paris Review, Furioso, The Saturday Review, Contact, Voices, Wake, The New Yorker, Measure, Berkeley, Synapse, Interim, Evergreen Review, Nadada, December, The Magazine, Nightshade, Galley Sail Review, Glass Hill, The Bridge, Twelfth Street,* and the *San Francisco Chronicle.*

BOOKS: *The New American Poetry,* ed. Donald Allen, Grove Press, 1960; *A New Folder,* ed. Daisy Aldan, New York, 1959; *The Playground,* 1949; *Musical Chairs,* 1950; and *The Ballad of Mad Jenny,* 1949, published by The Centaur Press, San Francisco; *An Almanac for Amorists,* Collection Merlin, Paris, 1955; *True & False Unicorn,* Grove Press, New York, 1957; *The Water Circle* and *Tidings,* Pterodactyl Press, San Francisco, 1965; *High Kukus,* The Jargon Society, North Carolina, 1969.

RECORDINGS: *The Bard and The Harper,* MEA, Sausalito, 1965



Library of Congress Catalog Number: 74-137209

Distributed by
Small Publishers' Company
Elm Street
Millerton, New York 12546

This project is supported by a grant from
the *National Endowment for the Arts*
in Washington, D.C., a Federal agency
created by Act of Congress in 1965.

Book design by Grabhorn-Hoyem, San Francisco.

*This book is for Suzanna*

She is as the Queen of the South Wind
who is said to come out of the East
like the rising dawn ripening to meet
He that is King of the North Wind
who reigns over the sun-sleeping West.

And where their dominions encounter
warm to his realm she will bring
tributes of the Earth and the Waters,
while he will bestow upon hers
a crown of gold Fire and bright Air.

Thereafter they shall roundly unite
their antipodal dawning and dusk
on one bed of all noons and nights
like the ancestral Sun and the Moon
upon the great wheel of the Stars.

*Wedding song for the film* Nuptiae (1969)
*music by Lou Harrison*

# Contents

III. SORROWS OF SCORPIO



IV. AN ALMANAC FOR AMORISTS

*Spring is a Virgin*



*Summer is a Bride*



*Autumn is a Mistress*

# *A Long Undressing*

## FOREWORD: I Am A Medium

I am not a Small, a Large, or an XL.
I am not long or short, raw or well done.
I am an M, a Medium, a Regular.
I am a Medium. But I like high mass and low dives,
sunsets and serpents, old wine and new wrinkles,
top drawers and getting to the bottom of things.

I am a third generation Californian.
My great grandfather was a scout with Fremont,
my grandmother was born in the Mother Lode,
my aunt served in the State Legislature.
When the sun was in Scorpio, the moon in Aries,
and the cusp of Virgo and Libra rising in 1913
I was born in the San Joaquin town of Modesto.

Most of my life has been lived in or near San Francisco
where my first books, plays and films were produced.
But also I have dwelt in the East
and I have visited the Far East and the Near East.
I live at present in Marin county with three persons:
my wife, my son and my daughter.

My grandfathers were bankers, and so was my father.
But my mother wanted me to become a surgeon.
However, one night when I was 3 years old
I was awakened by a glittering stranger
who told me I was a poet and always would be
and never to fear being alone or being laughed at.
That was my first meeting with my angel
who is the most interesting poet I have ever met.

My childhood passions were dancing and swimming,
circuses, amusement parks, movies, vaudeville,
the Book of Knowledge and the land of Oz.
Pet playthings: my toy theater, my magic lantern.
When I was 10 I was sent away to military school.
There my angel came to my rescue:
I fell madly in love with the English language.
(And also the captain of the baseball team.)
My favorite book is still Webster's Unabridged, 2nd ed.

At 12 I imitated all the Oxford Book of English Verse
and most of the Louis Untermeyer anthologies.
But ultimately I have learned more about poetry
from music and magic than from literature.
The clearest poetic memory of my years at Stanford:
the day Yvor Winters ordered me out of his class.
Poetry is a living adventure, not a literary problem.
(Other favorite books: Roget's Thesaurus, Tao Te Ching,
Mother Goose, Candide, The Marriage of Heaven and Hell.)

I have benefited from generous initiators.
Robert Duncan introduced me to the hermetic circle.
Madeline Gleason introduced me to poetry reading.
Adrian Wilson introduced me to fine printing.
Sidney Peterson introduced me to filmmaking.
Anais Nin introduced me to Anais Nin.
Joseph Henderson introduced me to C. G. Jung.
Alan Watts introduced me to joyous metaphysics.

I have enjoyed collaborations with many artists:
designers, performers, photographers, composers.
But I owe a special long salute to Kermit Sheets,

my sidekick and fellow conspirator for over 20 years.
In 1948 we started the Centaur Press in our basement
where Kermit printed handsome books of poetry.
His first: my verse play, *The Playground,*
which he also produced at the Interplayers theater.
Other Centaur books of mine from Kermit's hand:
*The Ballad of Mad Jenny* (in violet wrappers)
and *Musical Chairs* (with Lee Mullican drawings).

In this same period we were making experimental films
for Art in Cinema with the help of Frank Stauffacher.
Cinema has been for me a gratifying extension of poetry
since it can put imaginary toads into real gardens.
After my first adventure with *Mother's Day* (1948)
I acted *Jimmy*, Kermit created the role of *Loony Tom,*
together we shot and edited *Four in the Afternoon.*

During the early fifties we lived in Europe:
we made *The Pleasure Garden* film in London
thanks to Basil Wright, Lindsay Anderson & others,
and the book of *An Almanac for Amorists* in Paris
with little help from Alexander Trocchi at Merlin.
In a Paris hotel I wrote *True & False Unicorn*
which Marguerite Caetani first published in Rome.
A devoted friend and enthusiastic editor
she included much of my work in *Botteghe Oscure.*

As issued in book form by Grove Press in 1957
*True & False Unicorn* was designed by Jonathan Williams
whom I had met on my return to San Francisco in 1955.
Those were golden years for poets in the Bay Area
when public readings came into wide flower

and Donald Allen was gathering the New American Poetry.
I wrote *Whistling in the Labyrinth* then and *Tidings*
and worked with Kermit on productions of my plays:
*The Last Word, Where Helen Lies, The Rites of Women,*
*How Pleasant it is to Have Money,* and *Bedlam.*

I am a Medium. But I am also a Pagan,
an Anglican, a Buddhist and a Freethinker.
The poems of *Gods and Little Fishes* (1963)
resulted from my delight in Oriental philosophy.
Many of them were written for live performance
when I was doing an act with harpist Joel Andrews;
testament of this: our record, *The Bard & The Harper.*
In 1967 Jacques Ledoux of the Belgian Cinematheque
prodded my return to filmmaking: first result, *The Bed.*

So this book comes to an ending that is only a pause.
If *Musical Chairs* captures childhood's paradoxes
and the last poems are maturity's equivalent,
the painful middle years hold the alembic between.
Poetry, like love and religion, is the glorious
conjunction of both sense and nonsense.

The work here gathered does not by any means
include all the poems written between 1949 and 1969.
It comprises those grouped as books, published or not,
and those that I hope will not unduly embarass my angel.
For this collection many poems have been amended,
a few shelved, some sequences rearranged,
and much material printed for the first time.

A Medium is in the service of something larger than
his personal life, his craft, his published works.
I don't really know anything unless I can feel it.
If I like what it does, I go where it takes me.
I say only what it tells me and I try to stand by it.
And I don't have to believe it if I know that I know.
I am a Medium, and the Message from my angel says:
Attain the Inevitable. Allness is ripe.

*Mill Valley, July 4, 1970*

I

# *The Ballad of Mad Jenny*

## THE BALLAD OF MAD JENNY

*"Amo, ergo sum."*

Before I lie me down in my last martyrdom bed
I'll give a final tug to the threadbare knots
on the weaving it takes round to stitch up a life,
I'll try to pull together with the right hook and eye
which tuck of the tangle makes the dress for me
and where I'm to bury my poor tired hatchet.
For I've been at the spinning some mighty busy years
and I want to make sure my wig is on straight.

Now I know of no comfy waterproof closet
for hanging up the drenches and drying out the dregs.
Though I always kept my thumb up to pull in a plum,
though I still keep my wheelchair on a ten foot pole,
I have no cozy forecasts for a pat new world.

Enough hifalutin notions get picnicked in a sieve
by pouring out the soups of thick and thin,
but I never ever hoped to cook a snug ducky banquet
complete with a hatrack for each mind of a man.
Nor chart I now myself any smooth-floating passage.
I'm the potluck sort, who clears her own decks!
Wherever a warm boon may yet be blowing,
whatever sinky vessel comes due to depart me,
shall I know the captain sailing my misshapen sea?

And yet I have seen a lot I have seen
which maybe adds some total of the how things go,
for they seldom caught me napping anywhere along.
So all of you hereabouts, in the same boat or other,

if you want my scanty wisdom after all the heats are run,
and if you can listen, you may catch my old news.

It won't feature any cushion at a doll-baby nuptial,
no sofa on a racecourse, or a hummingbird throne,
but a bit what it's like to run agog headlong
head-up and head-on around the ring rosy,
around the ring rosy, around the stone treadmill,
to roll with God's circus and know how it's done.
If nonsense you're needing, I'm your wise girl!

Well sir, if I'm to state you no equivocal sense,
I'd need to begin with a riddle or so
pertaining to our feelings and the troubles thereof,
for that is the how it has always been a stickler
from the time I began and first howled for the moon.
Ah we've only to prattle and something falls down!
I'll begin as I'll end with the big riddle of all,
and maybe even yet a small frolic to solve it
will fool the wiseacres of our doubt-planting globe
with a rebirth of Venus, and Adonis to boot,
partaking of their myth bang-up in our midst
and showing us the trick of beating them to it.

But don't bet your hopes up too miracle high,
the best unexpected comes in not to expect
since there's some kind of limit to the neatest surprise.
I right from the start of my whirligig girleyhood
was quite never lacking recipes for doubt
nor knew how I'd know if ever I'd find
what I still try to know my heart will yet hold.
How that wishing unkeels me like a staggering lark!

And despite how I totter by the bed of my grave
why deny the sassy bird still tweaks in my breast?
I've been chirping, I thought me, for a long ago time
and still chirper am I when the time is unripe.
It's a hard row of pulling to sink an old dreadnaught!

I want, shall I say, what I always did want,
not a wanting to suit some ready-cut cloth.
To be more concise and take off my gloves,
I'm saying that the brightest big skirt I could spin
was to catch me that maintackle marksman at last
who would wizard my ship as the mate of all time
with a walking stick welcome to all outdoors
and a sea full of energy to seed my surprise.

It may be outrageous, perhaps, to your books
that the likes of a crone should be still on the skip
to bewitch even yet her real magnet of man,
but this is my deep irregardless desire
and if I can meet me a shipmate like this
I will make him the rosiest berth I possess,
I will shine his regattas, delight in his heydays.
For tell me what more really matters a whit
than to hatch our long aching to bloom to the full?
True love is the riddle that all of us quiz.

But how do you find it or how do you seek?
Where rides the prize of this wanting we wait?
Well, I've tried a few answers, I've kicked a few traces,
and I think that the odds are as even as not.
Though I can't rightly tell you the shape to describe him
nor what tune he will know his duet is for you,

he'll surely not trot forth full-hilt like a Zeus boy.
You'd wiser cock your eye for a cavalier aspirant.

When I was a girl and trapezes were lower
I had my share of dizzys and thuds.
Instead of acrobatics on a jump for joy
my somersaults caught me some neatly burned fingers.
As often as you I've had nettles in my nighttime
where breezy bold winds have stubbed a toe,
for the freer zeal runs the further it trips.
O the saving grace goes slippery through the touch!
Still I kept roping high for my true livewire.

When I was a girl there were men who rode handsome
and just as many who rode away.
No Cleopatrish world beater ever was I,
a run of the mill girl for all my looks.
Yet, as saucy I ripened while the boys trotted by,
don't think I missed my share of riding beside them.
There was one I recall for his alchemy smile,
one a jet falcon, one a bear of disorder,
and that singular sunburst who first melted my moons.
La I remember them all, God love them like I!

O I've made my mistakes, but they're my monkey business.
My talents have always run brightest when wild.
I'm not much a confector of sugarplum cure-alls
to gum a lad's works and pickle his ginger.
Nor I never was nifty at uplifting rubble,
nor at lifting Narcissus up to his mirror.
Yet I'll try every time to hew a man out
from the stuffing he is to the stuff he might be,

for the fellows are few in our world of cold feet
who come with their derring-do all ready-made.
A great slice of your riddling must be cut on what bias
you shall choose which Adonis to tend and to pace.

My own rapscallion darling didn't come to me dashing
from Lancelot's trade school or Lochinvar's tutor.
Besides are you sure you can match to his mettle?
You are much a warm mystery as he is to you.
The real quirk that will chain you to your unchainable hero
is a seed of some splendor and its need of your own.
Where the wedding takes root is a spring of your rebirth
and the warrior to be wombed is the man in your arms.
Shoo! I know a true thing, I'm not all a false nose!

Then weary me not with your goodbyes of blame
nor the taste of forgiveness that's worse than your gag,
I've a pearlier keepsake to bequeath to my clan.
A fie to the mockers who can only make wagwag!
For their kind of prattle all could fall down.
But I'm too far from port to fireproof my dreams
when I've sunk as many scandals as I've managed to launch
and nary found a mask any help to a shameface.
Uh! remorse was ever a hand-to-mouth maiden
and her noble shush shush puts the pinch on glee.
You don't cut to the core with a crutch for a knife,
you don't relish the egg with a shell on your tongue.

So what can I tell you I still would desire
or what tell myself will ever sail dearer
than a hurdle chase welcome to all outdoors?
Still handsome they ride, though the odds get remodeled,

and still floodtide am I to curtsey my heart,
while look at me now, with the squeaks in my knees.
I'm some quaky Diana, but I've not lost my quiver!
Hell take the handicaps, the detours, the tumbles,
I'd say it was worth it to keep the race running,
for peace is a death, of a kind of a kind.

Do you hear what I tell you will be as has been?
Are you anywhere near catching up with my drift?
It's not to be fickle, no, but it's not to lose faith
in the juiciest apple that can roll in your eye,
nor to balk at the orchard or the state of the sauce.
The nearest true lover is the farthest to find
and the wider you taste him the taller he grows.
How else will you match me to fill your own arms?

If you quarrel me quibbles to water my tonic,
since you're sure he won't come as I'm sure how he will,
it's plain as your fate that you'll never dare run
the risk of a rapture that could dazzle your wish.
Look sharper, old muddlehead, you may see what I mean!
For remedial frolics shall often be solved
when the magic can root where the moment strikes home.
Look fondly, young whisker, you may find what you see!
O the travel is lengthy, the journey short-lived,
but the magic will often, does often strike home.

Well, thus goes my riddle, and it's all of my news.
The threads bite off fine when the knots are in hand.
My rig may look wrinkled but it's worn me out well
all around the ring rosy, round and through the mill wheel.
And though here waits that last pillow to put my head down,
though here winds up my weaving, this old topknot still spins.

II.

# *Musical Chairs*

*Songs for Anxious Children*

TO WILLIAM BARRETT

*Being a child is no excuse.*
*Being a parent is a form of abuse.*

# *Nursery Problems*

## THE LITTLE READER'S FIRST RIDDLE

Where do the humans come from?
What are the humans begun from?
And how did I get here so small?

Though everyone somehow arrived in it
the world keeps on adding up odd.
If one and one make always two
can one and one make one at a time
and what's the connection with God?

O where did the humans jump from?
And how do the humans fall?

Though everyone lands on a mom and pop
there's a hitch to a family tree.
If two together have to marry
does one from two leave one to carry
and what is a stork to me?

Now where do the humans come from?
What are the humans sprung from?
And how did I get here at all?

## PAPA HAS A PIG

Papa has a pig.
And a big pig too.
Papa plays a piggy-toe that I can't do.
O Papa has the biggest pig you ever did see.
He gave only ten little piggies to me.
*Papa has the star of all the swine,*
*Papa shines stern in the sty.*

Papa goes to market.
And I stay home.
Papa doesn't tickle his toes all alone.
O Papa has the fattest pig you ever did feel.
My ten little piglets just pinch and squeal.
*Papa has the star of all the swine,*
*Papa shines stern in the sty.*

Papa has a pen.
And a big pen too.
Papa rides a piggy-back that I can't do.
O Papa stands out in the pig-feet race.
My ten little wiggles don't go any place.
*Papa has the star of all the swine.*
*Shine, Papa, shine in the sty.*

## MRS MOTHER HAS A NOSE

What a big nose Mrs Mother has,
the better to smell her dear.
Sniff sniff sniff it comes round the door,
detective of everything queer.

Two big noses Mrs Mother has,
the better to quell her dear.
"I smell something odd, I smell something bad,
what is that smell in here?"

Three big noses Mrs Mother has,
they grow and grow in the night.
Sniff sniff sniff her naughty naughty dear!
And she also can smell with her ears.

## LULLABY NEWS

Dear singular snookums, you're a beddie-bye sight.
It's a shame you have no partner to share your night.
But companions are expensive on Mama's account
at the big compartment store where babies come from.

It isn't Daddy's fault, he's a regular fellow.
His head goes right to sleep when it hits the pillow.
So your chum may be adopted at a slight discount
in the big compartment store where babies come from.

## BERCEUSE DÉLICIEUSE

Yummy diddle dumpling, come eat up my son.
Yummy diddle dumpling, eat my baby boy.
    He's a fat and tasty morsel
    to roll upon your tongue.
    Come devour my young joy.

Yummy tummy tidbit, come eat my daughter.
Yummy tummy tidbit, chew my baby girl.
    She's a rouncy bouncy pumpkin
    and as juicy as a plum.
    Come feast upon my pearl.

## NIGHTMARE RHYME

I was counting all the toes upon my fingers
five plus five plus six and a half—
*what ever happened to little dipper?*
and the trinkets in the sock went bang.

I was walking on my hands to count my footprints:
duck plus duck plus goose and a gull—
*what ever happened to little swallow?*
and the kittens in the sock went bang.

I counted all the toes on all my fingers:
five double five double zero and a half—
*what ever happened to little slipper?*
and the mittens in the sock went bang.

## JUNIOR'S PRAYER

Now I lay me down to sleep,
I pray the Lord to help me out.
I'm flat on my back and left alone,
so God bless nobody, please keep out.

If I should die and fall asleep
how will I run away from home?
If I should wake before I die
will I still be in the dark alone?

Now I lay me down to sleep.
But keep me awake, Lord, keep me awake!

## TICKLISH SUBJECT

Button button,
what good is my button?
Does it hold me together, fasten me right?
I pull it, I push it,
I try to unhitch it
and yet it just sticks in there tight.

Do Mommy and Poppy both have one?
Is it some sort of use when you grow up tall?
But what the hell do I do with it now
and why is it on my anatomy?

I'm beginning to learn
what things can be done
with the other parts that are part of me.
But button button,
what good is a button
that doesn't unbutton at all?

## MAMA IS GONE

O little lace collar
of the neck-squeeze size,
how ugh is the fear of the bug-bug trail?
*And Mama is gone, gone on ahead,*
*to the marvelous mah jong game.*

O little squeak shoes
on the pinchy tiptoe,
how long is the run through the tick-tock dark?
*And Mama is gone, gone on ahead,*
*to the marvelous mah jong game.*

O little velvet pants
squirming in the dismal,
how far upstairs can the pot be put?
*And Mama is gone, gone on ahead,*
*to the marvelous mah jong game.*

## THIS LITTLE DUCK

When will my little duck grow up big
so his wings will stay up
and his bill stick out?
Or how will he know what ducking's about?
    *This little duck isn't wild enough,*
    *this little duck is a dud.*

When will my duckling stand up straight
to spread out his tail
and take a long flight?
How will he ever be ducked out right?
    *This little duck isn't wild enough,*
    *this little duck is a dud.*

## THE DAYDREAMER'S PIE-EYED PIPER

Howdy do, wee wisher of the window-pane,
have you ever been to a popcorn festival?
Worn tingaling wings for your thinking cap?

Then come on, color up a red-letter calendar
with bluejackets, rockets, and pinky cream.
What zoom-zoom birds, catch as catch can!

O come on, run away to the popcorn festival.
No prune events there, no scoldy old parrots,
no hum and drum doghouse from home.

So let's go, wee wisher! Crack the window-pane!
Run quick and catch your own eagley bird
on the wing atingle with zim and boom!

# *Child's Play*

## THE HEIR OF THE PARSON

I don't like his looks and he don't like me,
but I'm a cowboy now and so is he.
So I'm gonna get my gun and go shoot Jesus,
I'm gonna shoot Jesus before he shoots me.

Pop says it's something you mustn't ever do,
that you can't shoot Jesus cause he's in Heaven
and you won't go to Heaven until you die
and you don't ever die till the right time to.

But I'm a good cowboy, I'll be tougher than he
and we'll fight this matter out for all to see.
I'm gonna get my gun and go shoot Jesus,
I'm gonna stop Jesus before he stops me.

## THE MOUTH-WATER KINGDOM

Sugar for Aunt Sally is the condiment to please.
She will rally juicy recipes for gooey cake and pie
in the angelfood kitchen where her gingerbread boys
button up their frosting and munch around the sky.

Sugar for my Aunty makes confectionery love.
She will sweeten her affection with sticky-finger fare
in the marshmallow oven where her lemon cream girls
dress in their meringuey tangs and permeate the air.

## GLADYS ON THE JUMP ROPE

One two three,
my bonnet has a bee.

Four five six,
my bag is full of tricks.

Seven eight nine,
my twinkle toe is shined.

Ten is the number
of the husbands in my heart.

Which one will count me
his true sweetheart?

## TAILS OUT OF SCHOOL

What, mother's ducky dear, what did you say?
What is this whisper of hide and peek?
O shame on shenanigans, tut tut tut!
Good little girls should be fooey and clean.

Whose wee pretty dimple is a wrinkle now?
Whose jack-in-the-box popped the whole shebang?
O fie on the dirty beans, spill spill spill!
No nice little girl plays gooey games.

Now, mother's goosey pet, how did it boomerang?
How did the hanky prank tit for tat?
Say your sorry whisper, bad baby sister,
but your tattle will be spanked just the same.

## CROSS-EYED JANE & WEEPY JIMMY

Said Cross-Eyed Jane to Weepy Jimmy,
"Yoo hoo, yoo hoo! Come over and play!
Come play King and Queen, I'll serve you tea.
I've a brand new crown, a crepe paper cape,
and half of my mother's butterscotch pie.
Please sit on my throne with me."

Said Weepy Jimmy to Cross-Eyed Jane,
"Boo hoo, go away! My bottom's too sore.
Go rule your own stool, I don't want your old teas.
No Queen's going to force down me anything more.
I won't really be King till I conquer Cascara
and just sit on a throne when I please."

## BIRD & BEE BUSINESS

Said Smarty Pants to Ishkabibble,
"Do you know what to do with a whozit?
Have you ever seen a youknowwhatImean?
And exactly how big gets a thingamajig
and what do you do if you lose it?"

Ishkabibble ran home to Hootnanny
and asked what she did with her whatzit
and if it should fit with a whatchamacallit.
But she did a rough job on his thingamabob
and spanked till he thought she would bust it.

## BACKYARD ELEGIES

1.
Poppa Cock Robin, who killed you?
You had bigger lungs than I
but it didn't help you.
When you got up to blow your top
they popped you in the stew.

So Poppa Cock Robin, what's the use?
To be a bigger bird than I
is asking for the noose.

I think I'll not grow up a lot
but stay a mum papoose.

2.
Teddy bear dear, can't you hug, can't you snuggle?
O dear! Teddy bear, did you give up the struggle?

3.
What do you need to react like a boy?
When do you feel like a real he man?
How can I act like a big tough baby
and still be myself as me as I can?

4.
I had a little bridge
and it had a little moon,
and everywhere the auto went
a star was sure to pop.

Until one day my moon-machine
got busted on the beam,
and everywhere the auto went
the little bridge fell plop.

5.

What are you doing here, little apple?
  The blossoms are faded,
  the leaves are no more,
  the cart's gone to market,
  the worm's in the core,
  God's left for the winter,
  the world's a backdoor.
Where are you rolling to, little apple?

## LITTLE BOY'S NASTY NEWS

A little boy's nasty news has a pal for his pimple.
Come out, my wart! Swell high, new swollen!
Bauble my fingers with tell-tale bumps.
The rewards of disorder are dense and spry.

But where did it happen? How did I do it?
Polliwogging sewers, fish-pond sliming?
The sandlot secret, wet with dirty beetles?
Will it hurt, will it itch, better than my hives?

The fruits of disorder are worry and maybe.
O come out, my wart! Grow wattle in the night!
Infect all my touch of infested nest.
A nasty boy's little news has brought the toad home.

## THE OUTFIELDER'S PET

What if he dawdles now?
What if my salamander lags in a snooze
and buries his nose in a lazy hole?
Just watch, ha!
Just wait till he crawls over
mounds of tall clover-cups, whish!
watch how he'll sprawl
over green and green
and shoosh! hit a high ball
into sky-high bluebells, wow!
way over and above
any dawdle lizard dugout
and right through all the peepholes
in your uppity bleachers,
ha ha! And how
will that do for a home-run zowie?

# *A Few Fables*

## THE TIGERS WERE TAKING A BATH

The tigers were taking a bath
in the midsummer garden of God.
The lions had suspended their wrath
to loll on seraphic sod.
The serpent had rolled up his tongue
and was picnicking under the tree
where the vulture angelically swung
bouncing a ball on his knee.
      And God saw that it was good
      (though not surprising)

But the humans arrived in alarm
to find paradise set up so wrong.
They tidied the trespassers' harm
and bounced those who did not belong.
They retuned the tiger to roar,
reinfected the serpent's kiss,
of the lion they requested fresh gore
and offered the vulture their bliss.
      And God saw that it was Good
      (though not surprising)

## THE ANGEL-BIRD TIDIES UP

The angel-bird came by on a peekaboo night
to sweep up the decimals in our slumber murk,
and took us for a ride on a feather-duster flag
shaking out our dreams of all their logarithm work.

Ouch, said the owl-chainer, what's the idea?
We were smidgin-collecting nicely till he came along.
With our night-hooks ready for toting up a catch
we were baiting little squirms who went to sleep wrong.

But the angel-bird picked up where the dream left off
and took us for a ride on a slick and whistle kite.
He aired out all the sky to erase the blackboard spooks,
and on the way around the moon our fractions came out right.

Damn, said the owl-chainer, this night shift is too unpredictable.

## HAUNTED HOMEWORK

They crawl conglomerate under every floor,
the squat root-snippers in tidbit attire.
Listen, how they thwack the gardener's room!

Zigzag on the roof prowl the petal-choppers too,
leaking whooping cough seeds from sick vest pockets.
Hush, hear the thin feet thicken by the hour!

Hobnobby with goblins they congregate the hall,
the squint house-chippers in their wall-bending caps.
Sssh, outside the door they are pinching up the stairs!

## THE SWEET-TOOTH WITCH

I've an appetite for curls and dimples in a chin.
Awhiz through the midnight stratospherey
on my lickety spittle I zeppelin,
pursuing little girls who are good as gold
to cook them up for supper in my eerie.

I marinate and lard them,
I roast their thin-skin hides,
I bake a custard pudding
of their saccharine insides,
and since they have no spines at all
I pickle their backsides.

I love a dainty blush and neatly washed ears.
Mother's darling helpers, Daddy's perfect dears,
nice proper prissies who never have a wicked wish,
all good little girls who do what they're told
are just my dish .

## PERAMBULATOR PERILS

Is it being so wise to air your child in a public park?
Sweet-smelling ambush thrives in a landscaped loam
on green worms, long blue flies, snakes little snakes.

Does it seem a prize to share your babe with a subtle lark?
Tweet-throated birdies bide in a hornet zone
of nets and gnats, beetle bones, snakes little snakes.

Is it being so wise to snare your doll in a public dark?
Neat-eating bugbears connive in a leafy home
with mean moths, big shoo flies, snakes little snakes.

## MR SOMETHING-OR-OTHER

He owned a goose and an apple tree,
two foods he liked best in the world.
But every ripe apple that fell to the ground
his goose got up early to eat.
*O which shall I keep:*
*the bird or the fruit?*

He built a fence round his apple tree,
his goose flew over before he was up.
He hung a net below the boughs,
she worked all night and pulled it down.
*O which shall I keep:*
*the bird or the fruit?*

He chopped to the ground his apple tree,
one food he liked best in the world.
But his goose in anger flew away
and he sat alone in his yard.
*O which shall I keep:*
*the bird or the fruit?*

## MRS MIDAS

Cold Mrs Midas had a big gold bag,
*two bits four bits tucked in the hay,*
but she dressed her daughter in a dirty rag
so instead of a deb the girl looked a hag.
*A penny is a penny any time of day.*

She refused to give pocket money to her son,
*two bits four bits tucked in the hay,*
she sewed up his pockets one by one
and shipped him off to beg in Galveston.
*A penny is a penny any time of day.*

Her husband was found of eating spumoni,
*two bits four bits tucked in the hay,*
so she got a divorce for a lot of alimony
and now he can't afford to boil macaroni.
*A penny is a penny any time of day.*

The bag of Mrs Midas grew so comfortably wide,
*two bits four bits tucked in the hay,*
that to save herself rent she moved inside,
and there, my dears, is where she died.
*A penny is a penny any time of day.*

## THE WEDDING OF THE CAT AND THE CANARY

No carnivorous occasion gave me cause to rejoice
till that feast when my panther altered his voice
by catching my thrush, which got stuck in his throat
and there coloraturas a double high note.

My once snarling beast has dropped his old trait
and now plays obbligato to oblige his new mate,
so in jungle resplendence my bird tweets more spry,
enarmored she runs more chromatic to fly.

With claws on her wings and sure-footed toes,
a purr to her trilling and fur on her nose,
my thrush now has teeth for the leap of her flight
to sing sweet duets of hybrid delight.

## JUNGLE LULLABY

Mammy's put her black-eyed pea to bed.
Snooze, baby sugarpuss, snooze if you can,
this neighborhood is humid and noisy too.
Boo boo! toots the all night bugaboo band.

The macaw shrieks in the papaw tree
(it's the usual spooky hullaballoo)
the agouti to the ocelot eek! parakeet!
the crocodile squawks at the kinkajou.

Damp in the swamp the flamingo sniffles,
"Unhealthy place for a family tree!
The habits of a habitat don't endear it to me,
I'm dank in the knees, kerchoo!"

Someday Mammy's gonna move to town,
as soon as the zoo has a vacancy.
A dry apartment in a big city, whee! free!
and poo to these all night jungle blues.

## THE GOOD RODEO FAIRY

Very rough and tumble those root-tooting rustlers
had been ambushing our valley from hill to hill,
while we hoe-down lovers were growing weary
jumping out of step to skip their kill.

Then the Good Rodeo Fairy rode over our cloud
all bounce and lilting on a round-up trip,
with his star-saddled pinto, spiffy ten-gallon,
and neatly sharp-shooting tricks on his hip.

In the nick of time he lassoed with a trounce
the low-down villains who had stubbed our toes.
So circular sweetly again we have tempo
and plenty of room for our pretty heigh-hos.

# *Older Girls & Boys*

## ROBIN HOOD'S OTHER NEPHEW

Tackle the consequence straightly, say I.
My gunwale is ready to sail up the moon
to arm and embark a bang-up armada
of all the stray archers who dream in the noon.

I have lifeboats to sequel, I am equal, say I,
to the swiftest and brisk your tricksters can wield.
Conceal what they will in their slingshot ambush,
I have arrow wings growing to pierce any shield.

Such damage I'll do to these miniature gorgons
who prickle and buckle and spit on my pie.
Their tariffs and tickets are brain dust gone sticky.
O off with their scalp disease quickly, say I.

So aloft in the noonday I launch for the moon
to polish my aim at your bull-penny eye.
Then watch when my archers give pull and take swoop,
watch the whole shooting match fly, say I.

## MISS SAUCEBOX

Are you my sweet pea?
Have you come to tickle me?
Will you pinch my cherry pie?
      Be a bold boy!

Kiss me quick and make me jump,
kiss me quick and take my trump,
try a lick of sugar lump,
      I'm a tasty toy!

Ho, hello,
have you come to tickle me
with drumstick, match trick?
      Be a bold boy!

## PARIS STREET SONGS

I.

   Geraldine, Geraldine,
she's not pretty, she's not clean,
plays with the boys and lets them play,
stays out all night on Saturday,
she'll never lunch at the Elysée.
   Geraldine, Geraldine
will not learn a proper dance,
never wears her underpants,
she's a blot on the name of France,
she's not pretty, she's not clean,
   O I envy Geraldine!

2.

Jean and Jeannot and Jean-Michel
three little angels out for hell
larked up the quai, lurked down the rue
looking for jokes to say and to do,
    scrambled down the Metro
    scribbled up a wall
    smoked a Gauloise butt
    nosing through Les Halles—
peeked at the long, poked at the short
peepeed and pooed and piddled for sport
from Menilmontant to the Tour Eiffel,
Jean and Jeannot and Jean-Michel.

## THE HAPPY PETTY THIEF

I took what I wanted,
I filched all I wished.
I fled with the loot
in a small silver dish.

Now daily I dust off
the nestegg I stole,
and sleep on it nightly
where I dug it a hole.

I sweep what I swiped,
I shall keep it real neat.
I've no reason to spend it,
my career is complete.

## THE LANDLUBBER'S CHILD

As for considering a cruise with that cloud-rocking captain
beckoning at me from the beam of the sky,
where's the convenience of sailing on a high flighty ark?

Any down to earth boatman with hot broth and fishhooks
would be welcome to arrange an itinerary.
But what could guarantee solid holiday comfort
when the navigating tactics are all up in the airy?

As for booking a passage with such a high and mighty pilot
reckoning fathoms from a seam in the sky,—why,
there's not even a railing round his fly-by-night ark!

## BEYOND HER DEPTH

'I peeked at the sea.
And the sea piqued me.
What a lot of rustle-tussle
swish-wash and spitty-boom!
Why can't the sea relax and be
as simple, say, as A or B?'

With which that angry ugly hokey-pokey girl
named Lulubelle O'Connor from Yuba City
took a tuck in her ticklepin
hitched her middle up higher than usualdom
and tripped herself back to very dry land
in a huff-bundle.

She never went to see again,
no, not she.
She stuck her needle deep in the hay
determined to stay
perfectly content with B or A.

## HOUSEHOLD PETS

1.

He meddles and muddles in everything,
that puddly poodle, that puppy piddler.
What a floor, what a bore!
Put your peasey in a porridge pot, please—
this is not a pool room.
O what a pissy pup!

2.

Skat, Herr Meow, do you hear me now,
no more of your caterwaul under my skirt!
O that saucy old pussy,
how he bosses me about, howling for his nip.
Skat, sassy cat, old licky-fur, skit and skedaddle
or back in the bag go you!

## THE LADY OF THE HOUSE

All of my stockings have snagged a run,
the wallpaper peeled off the hall,
my very best tooth has got to be pulled
and the moths have devoured my stole.
    It's a horrible plight for me!

The identical twins have divvied the cook,
my daughter has flunked out in French,
and nothing came back from the Chinese wash
but somebody else's winding sheet.
    What a horrid disorder to be!

Grandmother's parrot bit off her thimble,
the hot water heater has burst,
my husband has left me, the cellar is flooded,
and my curtains don't match my couch.
    I'm a horrible state to see!

## THE SHEPHERD'S URBAN DAUGHTER

Mary has lost her childhood lamb,
she wants the fleece back as pure as it was,
but her pretty bo peep has broken down
and she can't tell a sheep from what a goat does.
    *This is the norm, this is the norm,*
    *this is the way it goes, madam.*

She's confused about all the sheep she has known:
if they had tails and where they grew
and whose was whose and how to know
and which was which and what she should do.
    *This is the norm, this is the norm,*
    *this is the way it goes, madam.*

She is gathering old wool together now.
With no flock to count, no pastoral crook,
she lies awake nights and knits her brow,
and her doctor is writing it down in a book.
    *This is the norm, this is the norm,*
    *this is the way it goes, madam.*

## THE LIGHTHOUSE KEEPER'S OFFSPRING

Storms once hurled my howls about,
but now no traumas worry me.
I the skiff that hugged safe harbor
find no harbor save the sea.

And there is where I'll choose to bed,
stretching out on rolling tide.
There my boat shall aim its sailing,
there will I like Christmas glide.

Gods unknown, O god of racing,
grace me fleets to steer my own.
If free I can, if me I can,
such as this my bold will go:

Straight across the world's old sorrow,
lightly rigged for shipshape seas,
and all of earth's dry murder thrown
overboard with ease.

# *Facts of Life*

## FRUITS OF EXPERIENCE

1.

Pomegranates come from red hot pearls.
Cherries are the hearts of baby girls.
Persimmons come up on the bosom of dawn.
Plums fill the sky when the day is gone.
Pineapples grow on the heads of kings.
Bananas are nothing but naughty things.

2.

A serious person is a serious business
and serious business is a serious thing
and serious things are very serious
and taken seriously are dead serious
and nothing is as serious as a serious person
and a serious person is seriously dead.

3.

A cop says No
a priest says No
but a little boy hardly ever.
Generals go by
and Popes go by
but little boys last forever.

## HELPFUL KNOWLEDGE

60 seconds make a minute,
60 minutes take an hour,
60 pounds fill a bushel of wheat
and nearly 200 a barrel of flour.

7 days take a week,
52 weeks make a year,
2 gallons go into a peck
and 31 into a barrel of beer.

24 sheets make a quire,
20 quires take a ream,
9 square feet are 3 feet square
and 63 gallons a hogshead of cream.

2 radii make a diameter,
3-point-plus takes care of pi,
56 pounds fill a firkin of butter
as well as a bushel of corn or rye.

## GEOGRAPHY LESSON

Once upon a time table
I took a lively trip.
At half past five I left for Spain
and got to Crete by six
  (without a hitch or slip).

To Switzerland I rode a boat,
to Mandalay a bus,
but since they both set off at once
I went the Swedish route
   (by way of hit and miss).

Rome, Peru and Ottawa
I passed through very quick,
so at Istanbul I booked a mule
and flew back home instead
   (and never missed a trick).

## HISTORY LESSON

*Everything had to be this way,*
*nothing could be every way.*
He searched with his bucket tightly sealed
tiptoe around the mountain,
and found no pool with roof of steel
in which to bide his trout.

*Nothing has to be this way,*
*everything can be any way.*
Straight up the road of starving cats
marches the true-eyed pilgrim,
a mountaineer with a deep sea net
and field flowers in his mouth.

## FISHING LESSON

Angles to angling
as wish is to fish.
Which will you catch? Will it catch on?
Bait is to angle
as wish is to which.
And a watery watch is to look upon.

Polecat puts fishpole
right down the line.
No confusable hatch to which it on.
Not taddypoles. Not cattytails.
Fish is a fish.
And a catch is what you hook upon.

## BIG CRADLE SONG

    Father Sun
    Mother Moon
how was your union blest?
    Golden Cock
    Silver Hen
what was the egg in your nest?

    Lord of Day
    Lady Night
is the babe in your arms the earth?
    Father Sun
    Mother Moon
do you now regret its birth?

## GENESIS OF VOWELS

A is to begin with, and A began with Adam.
E is to proceed with, and Eve was her name.
I is what they ended with, and I of course is me.
O is how they did it, O over O and over.
U is what undid them, underneath the game.
    For Y was added to the act.
    Adamant is Y.
    Even crawling inside O
    it yowls at U and I.

## ADAGES

There's no way around
what is already around
but there's plenty of room inside.

***

It's a sad fate to drown in a well gone dry
by holding one's nose and biting one's tongue.

***

What you have to swallow
doesn't have to go down
without a peep.

***

Tannhauser too was once a tot with a bottle.
And even Venus began with a hot toddle.

***

A noisy big nose is a nuisancy diehard,
but in the long run will blow itself out
while wee modester winds breathe on.

***

By all means, try all means.

## HAPPY ENDING

Promise, snickelfritz, never put away your bold.
Juggle all the risks at hand, as handsome does.
Manage your own magic with pep and aplomb.
Ignore the old bodies always busy with their buzz.
*You're never as bad as they say, O they!*

Dump out the lead, the cold fears in your boots.
With a warmy ha ha keep stirring your stumps.
Audacity's the buddy for your long-term trip.
Don't waste a single sorry on the tch tch frumps.
*You're never as bad as they say, O they!*
*You're never as bad as they say.*

III

# *Sorrows of Scorpio*

FOR ANAIS NIN

*To have been lanced,*
*the blade run through the very center,*
*to be beginning to grow rot:*
*when what I sought (or thought)*
*was a beginning to go running*
*with flowing blade and pennant for the sunlight dance.*

*But the sword-race stumbled at the double quick.*
*O rage inrage of the fumbled step—*
*to have sought for grace and running*
*on a gargoyle's foot!*
*The old totem grins new outrage*
*carved from the heart of my limp.*

## THE GRAVITY OF SPILT MILK

What's in a nightmare as brisk and as light
as all of man's mansions that glitter upright?
And the once-weeping mothers have nothing to grieve.

Wakeful watched me all the night
the ogre of my travesties:
shameless waited at the lock,
a teardrop mallet on his knee.
O see how he smiles and wigwags at me!

That stranger in his coatless sleeve
struck my pretty while she slept,
leaving me only my worry clock
so I'd be the waker who wept.
O see how he smiles and wigwags the tale!

What fancy can matter or scatter what glee
if all of man's memory makes water on me?
And the once-weeping mothers have no more to wail.

## BRIDGE TO THE INNERMOST FOREST

I could not match the labels where the span held the patch
in its doubling of layers on the cables of starch.
For the cape on the arch of the statuary perch
excluded all question of door and path.

I would cover it with spank or with shield or with glass,
but the multiforming gate that would never fix

kept hedging its formula for the wiry copse.
And the tensity of pitch could never be disguised.

I could not catch and mix the meaning of this glen
where the wiser and the meager had already lain.
For the capture of the curtain's thistling stone
excluded all answer of lock and hinge.

I would cover it with fear or with plaster or with noose,
but the multiforming gate would admit of no release
nor admire an oasis in the squamous woods.
And the density of ditch could never be surmised.

## THE ROADS TO THE CROSSROADS

Like the weathercock wobbling his back and forth
on my route of schisms I have turned tick-tock.

Blown down the sidetracks, misled by my wall eye,
in the right grave of gravity I wooed the blind hag.

Down the left-handed ditch lie my touch-and-go dolls,
their socketless pillows embered into rock.

At the straight-forward milestone Aphrodite's garden
still crannies bride-flowers among burnt slag.

Shall ever I weather to that uprighted orchard
where my cross grows greening round the clock?

## THE MADMAN'S HOUSE

Slippers he made me,
and where the high horn lay
he opened a madhouse and I walked in.

'Turn not! Trust not any who point that way!
For overshoes ache when brightest made
and no one returns from there or them!'

I stopped where I stepped, sleep I dared not,
I waited awake—then was banged overside
by shepherd that grew utter beast on a cord.
Lo! there was acne all over my wings
and sick how I dreaded the core of my hood.
I swung mercy wildly and drunk waded on.

'See! no one returns from there or them!
The mockers of moon, all slit for the ride,
come sleekly come oafish come outsize or shorn.
No matter what magic, what worry you spell,
no answer sees certain, no dancer seems brave,
none smiles or none aids you. All cohorts askew!'

Thus mock rode my saddle, I fumbled, I tripped,
shame chased my blunder, till tumbling uphill
I kicked the shoe off... O! My heart lost its mind.

Slippers he made me,
and where the high horn lay
he closed up the madhouse and I stayed in.

## IN THE SANITARIUM

How did I arrive in this chill and gutted museum?
The guide provided by the agency
had skipped at the first frontier.

Gadgets, pellets, the extra wool wadding
made no difference:
chronic and toxic continued to prove mortal.

Having presented in detail the nature of my case,
I was interrupted. He said, bluntly,
"It is not worth more than a dollar an hour."

Treatment of the shock:
what to shut off, which draft the most deadly?
The smaller the night hours the larger the scissors!

Is all of man's life a convalescence?
To spend one more night here is unbearable.
"Yes," said the nurse, "but imperative."

## LIKENESS OF THE WEASEL

Walls have fallen against my searchlight
and dusk is the color of my seeing.

Shall I pocket my tempest of appalling dream,
print it in cold face for glum edition?

*Likeness of the weasel*
*nibbling the bush-tit,*
*so frets the old fire under fur.*

Palls have fallen upon my fuses
and dusk is the color of my semen.

Balls! Rocket a rainbow of ungalled dream,
mint it in bold face for plummet issue!

*Likeness of the weasel*
*nibbling the bush-tit,*
*O sweat out the fur under fire.*

## WRONG SONGS

I.

Something is wrong
is wrong again
but something is always wrong.
Fever burns strong
it blinds again
and the mind dies short of breath.

Something is wrong
is long is dread
if the night sits blank on the noon.
But something is
always something wrong
when the mind lies down by the dead.

Hate hides deeper
behind love's face
and fever strangulates song
when something is wrong
is strong as death
when something is always wrong.

2.

O how swift the traps begin to grow
underneath the circulating smirks and gowns,
and all around the lamps snip snap
and the flags come down.

What was feathered for a bird-burst
fungus rusts and weather drowns,
weights fall hefty all for dust,
pull pull the magics down.

Round and round O all around
snares unwind and baitings bristle,
night-nets pull tall wish aground
and cages shut the wonders down.

3.

After loving is after
after before is late,
no hour no gate:

twist and tug it and wrench—
the net will hold
the knots will hold you
entangled intrenched—

when loving is after
and before is late,
after before is hate.

4.
Thorns will be worn for the masquerade kill:
knot the thistle tight underneath your chin.
Nettle-lined vest for the spine's old chill,
pin up the knees where the blood runs thin.
Stings on your fingers and welts on your toes,
burrs for your bottom sharpening the itch,
bifocal bramble-patch clamped to your nose:
thorns will be worn stitch by stitch.

Skewer new stigmata to the roots of the hair,
pierce the ear with needlepoints inch by inch.
Briery for tongue and prickly-heat prepare,
barb the tender nerve where the old shoes pinch.
Pangs for your cheeks and dagger for your eye,
porcupine your finery quill by quill,
bleeding-heart medals dress you up to die:
thorns will be worn for the masquerade kill.

## THE ASPICKED LOVERS

*A Descriptive Problem Play*

SCENE I
The questing mind must be checked at the door.
How thin the air! How soft the static!
Dry jelly in which all objects sit.
No key questions please about the cupboard.

Yet what is this hunger met in the eyes?
Was I expected to bring extra cookies?
Such savor of water the menus promise.
And no rapier to test the custard consistency.

Merely a girlish greed for new toys?
(Take note of the anchored hobby horse,
the chubby child's nibbled thumb,
the bounce of the careful hoops.)

Or a guileless cannibal welcome?
So many framed photos, such a wide hatrack.
Would it have been better to have stayed home
in the stomach of my own trap?

SCENE 2

Everyone on the beach has a squirming pillow.
And in the resort hotel, drawn with the blinds,
steam heat, alcohol, aspirin.
Danger! A weekend for a lifetime.

But everything is very very nice.
What magic? Was it cold chemistry?
Or which did she want?
So much flubdub over false licorice.

How glibly ravel uneasy passions,
how easily treachery habituates!
And whose, if not one's own?
Me in my threadbare lifebelt!

Her releasing grasp: 'You are free to go—'
Back to my colder danger?
Old habitudes of solitary soup?
The choices of despair are a bag of bones.

Scene 3
Question here the domestic arrangements.

Upholstered lair for naked lion,
propriety for the crooked eagle?
More likely a leash on the housebroken cat
and permanent cover over the canary.

Then why does my gloved hand twangtwang
repeats on a harp of compromise?
Corruptible! With consequences.
No wonder my nests are dinky.

Yet I sicken on shut-in games.
This nausea is served on ice.
Still the dainty sleeping pill!
Still the midnight snack, souring in syrup!

O for a genuine broken leg!

Scene 4
Bloody: the color of mud.
Mud over everything. Our feet deep.
But worst of all: my wavering knife.
To marmalade even the death throe!

I too was wound, being murderer.
But not this martyr on a spurious cross.
Hungry eyes still hungry for more wounds,
her bleeding eyes still hungry for my blood!

No pity. No victory.
To each his snare,
to each his own peccable quagmire.
To both—the sticky accusing finger.

## CALL FOR A DESPERATE MEASURE

So are we all, in our labyrinths.
Is inert sorrow plugged in to stay?
A plow to break the otiose, please!
For a furbelow of freedom if nothing more.

No breathing room in these lap-dog kennels?
Merely speedier crutches of newer driftwood
to go hopping again around the mirrors
with a woodener pout to whittle at?

A little arson, please, a little aerification
to dare some miracle of small surprises!
At least a bauble, at least!
Or so are we stalled, in our labyrinths.

## L'APRÈS-MIDI D'UN WERTHER

Sumptuous or not, the terraces for summer ribaldry
revive the odor of dead desire.
Under the limes an old ouch lurks out
whether hammock or mimosa skip the air.

Seldom very seldom hornets remain at rest
in the well-swept corners of hot rotting green.
So it is O only apparently a solace,
this thick garden sunshine sticky with seed.

Ouched to reflower by a ribald summary,
old fingertipping perfumes poison the hands.
And, sumptuous or not, afternoon embraces clutch a chill:
fresh heats cannot bewitch love's cold demand.

## A FORCED SOJOURN IN MORIBUNDIA

Much as I would like to bake a nightingale pie
there seems to be no perch for juicy feathers
in this unseeded area,
deodorized being the chlorophyll
and shrunk the twigs.

Did you notice the basket-weaver's fingers?
They were woven into the design:
the slivered skin in arabesque interlocked the nails.
And the price was marked down,
for ordinary casket use.

Much as I would like to revise the local menu
songbird cooks are in ill repute.
These surgeons prefer the wrong sugarcoats.
Not the faintest copy of Utopian greenery,
nor even a tastier poisoned biscuit.

Citizens,
are your bellies pre-shrunk to fit the famine?

## THE AUTUMNAL ASTROLOGER'S PRAYER

O Lord Scorpio, of my deported realm,
all fusty-flung lags my zodiac,
I have lost the active octave of my moon.
Dim fits the fuse of my indirect circuit
to the genital font of the sun:
look! my starry armada gone aground.

O daytime Minister of sluggish deeps,
of abattoir, bog, and ash,
where lifts the navigation of your twilight Eagle
for all my steep drifts and variance?
What sinewy compass can your Serpent spin
to re-outfit my maritime firmament?

Once I was adept at pirating Neptune,
at bedecking the mermaids in Jupiter's fleet,
I could skipper any Venus on a trine-shaped sea.
But now, dismantled, dark in this drydock,
how shall I rescue and recrown with fire
the diamond navies of my night?

IV

# *An Almanac for Amorists*

FOR ESTO BROUGHTON

*"All seasons are love seasons"*

# *Spring is a Virgin*

## A ROUND FOR PRINCESS PRINTEMPS

Spring<br>
   spring<br>
      runs round a green riddle,<br>
follows a round robin cruel and gay.<br>
   The virgins of April<br>
   heed the call of the leapfrog<br>
and go on a roundtrip till the middle of May—<br>
   for the sons of Apollo<br>
   rush out to shoot apples<br>
around the round riddle<br>
           hey diddle<br>
               hooray!

## THE ORPHAN GIRL IN THE PLEASURE GARDEN

Strangers we are, the world and I—<br>
curious strangers passing by.<br>
My heart is locked up like a wishbone dry<br>
the world's pretty strangers touch and go by.<br>
  *O where is the key to the golden city?*<br>
  *And the taste of the honey in the moon?*

Curious strangers, the world and I.
Is there no stranger curious for me—
with a moon in his pocket and a golden key?
For my heart is locked up and I might die
with only a wishbone old and dry.
    *O who has the key to the golden city?*
    *And the taste of the honey in the moon?*

## THE CLEVER TROUBADOUR OF AMORET COUNTRY

Happiest am I when my Ada is most tongue-tied
and her dairydell bushes bulge fat with birds,
for then I can whistle as fine as any Shelley,
be full of fancy talk without spelling out the words.
    I'm a lightfoot buckaroo on a beehop pace
    and Delicate Crazy is my hometown.

Prettiest is Beulah when she is most illiterate
and her berries are baked all sweet into pies,
for then I go courting as slick as any Byron,
I rollick foolish talk and feel I'm sitting very wise.
    I'm a tricky toodledoo for a cock and bull race
    and Delicate Crazy is my hometown.

Tempting best is Cleo when awe has struck her dumbest
and her starchy wash hangs a white tent on the lines,
for then I sing niftier than any old Shakespeare,
with a mouth full of kisses I write my valentines.
    I'm the poetical winner of the boy and girl chase
    and Delicate Crazy is my hometown.

## THE GARDENER'S SON

I have cap, I have trouser,
I have tears yet to learn
on mountain and meadow
where foxes still woo.
I have shovel and planting
for a loam way to travel,
till I bed a wild dove
when the rose is new.
*Pure will blow my love,*
*honeyed will she be :*
*O what beautifying of the bee !*

Then I shall snip the link
of the snail-sender's shrink
and the statue with clean sleeves,
I shall skip the foxes too.
So mock not my greensleeves,
for I will queen a kingdom
I will mate a ringdove
when the rose is new.
*Pure will blow my love,*
*honeyed will she be :*
*O what beautifying of the bee !*

## ARIA FOR ADONIS, SOTTO VOCE

Lover (O loveliest word)
One O inflammable wonder
in cool flower . . .

How sweats lobster brain for a trumpet—
How aches leopard mask to burst into bird—
How thaws the frost flesh, cracks icicled heart,
quakes wide the whole bodily earth—Now
to bloom Alp, erupt sea, and God dance!

O loveliest (not word) One
world to be burned in wonder
of cool flower . . .

## A NUMBER OF SURPRISES FOR JIMMY

Four corners there were to the round round world.
I expected love in more than three.
But the first two I stood in proved to be
a seat for the self and a shelf for the me.

With two corners left to the round round world
I expected love in one out of four.
But the last two I stepped in proved to be
a dunce-capping dream and a trap in the floor.

Four corners there are to the round round world
but the number to count on has figures galore.
When I rounded a corner love did not foresee
the world squared itself and transfigured me.

# *Summer is a Bride*

## PSYCHE TO CUPID: HER DITTY

Come dally me, darling, dally me with kisses,
loiter me with lingers while the Romes all burn.
Carouse me, my ducky, O tousle my wishes,
I will overabundantly romp in return.
    Sing nimble, sing careless
    of impulsive exuberance,
    sing loud the disgraces of exuberant love.

The skies can roll downhill for all I shall care
if you'll rumple my willingness tempting and sweet.
Come loll me, O dally me thoroughly rare,
I will romp and reward you a comparable treat.
    Sing nimble, sing careless
    of impulsive exuberance,
    sing loud the disgraces of exuberant love.

## EPITHALAMION OF OLD UNCLE OVID

Merry fine lads grow fewer each day
and the sturdier ones make haste to wed,
so it's far between and it's way roundabout
when it comes to that specially well-met fellow
who will row you away in a strong houseboat,
who will row past the land of the dead.

The way to any wedding
doesn't take a ready road
through the bumpy hills of desire,
but the moon keeps its honey in a pot of gold,
the honey in the moon runs hot.

Good pretty girls grow older each day
and the shrewder ones take the first to wed,
so it's hit or miss but a sharp lookout
for that one shepherdess on a seaworthy pillow
who will steer your daring like a jewel afloat,
who will smile down the land of the dead.

The route to wedding treasure
doesn't go an easy map
through the zigzag forest of the heart,
but the moon keeps its honey in a pot of gold,
the honey in the moon runs hot.

## THE ICE CREAM GIRL IN THE PLAYGROUND

O laughing, my lover, where come you, where lie?
I could lap you so lovely, I care not to die.

O loving, my laugher, where come you, where lie?
I could lip you so lively, I can bear not to die.

Come tense me, my due love, tense me and claim:
The world's bloody raiment weaves me a chain.

Come clench me, my new love, propensity claim:
The oxen of murder are calling my name.

O densely, my true love, come ripe and renew:
The aged are endless, the newborn are true.

## DUET FOR A BLIND DATE

How do you do, miss maiden,
and how do I dance with you?
In view of the criss-cross eye of the moon,
do you mind if I ask, Who are you?

*I would if I could, but I can't.*
*I'm not always myself, you know.*

But many a duo can double as one
if it crosses its I with its me.
From my point of view of the kiss-eyed moon,
which one is you and who's thee?

*I could if I would, but I won't.*
*I'm not always myself, you know.*

But all the world's ones comes out by twos
for a four-legged waltz of whom and who.
By the double-cross moon, do you mind if I ask,
Who who, miss maiden, are you?

*I should if I did, but I shan't.*
*I'm not always myself, you know.*

## THE GIRL WITH THE BEADY BLACK EYES

She was my honey baby, she sure was my delight
    with her beautiful beady black eyes.
I met her in Modesto in the middle of the night
    when the old hotel burned down.

Her name was Ida Lee, she stood blushing in a fright
    with her beautiful beady black eyes.
She had come from San Francisco just to pass the night
    but the old hotel burned down.

In her lace and pinky nightgown she looked a rosy sight
    with her beautiful beady black eyes.
I saved her from the flames in the middle of the night
    when the old hotel burned down.

She is still my honey babe, though her hair is turning white
    with her beautiful beady black eyes.
In our San Francisco home we often laugh about the night
    when the old hotel burned down,
        when the whole town burned to hell.

## THE PSALM OF ST. PRIAPUS

*Lion of my sun, my fiery joy,*
*thou art my maker and my destroyer.*
*Thy flowering rod is the fact of Heaven,*
*thy bursting seed is the act of God.*

Let me clasp thy soul, this golden flower!
To caress its power is the glory of my earth.
Let me do it worship, let my lips anoint it.
This is the temple of my Holy Ghost.

Let me drink deep of thy sacred fountain
its bitter-sweet honey-hot milk of love.
Let me lie drunken at thy throbbing spring.
This is the mouth and the taste of God.

Set me afire with it, burn my heart alight.
Thy torch of rapture all my genesis is.
Nail me aflame to thy fertile cross of fire.
Hallowed be my lion, my blazing Host!

*Lion of my sun, my fiery joy,*
*thou art my maker and my destroyer.*
*Thy flowering rod is the fact of Heaven,*
*thy bursting seed is the act of God.*

# *Autumn is a Mistress*

## A LAD FROM THE COLD COUNTRY

When I dwelt in the wood in a wind-cracked hut,
(at a waterwheel pinch the rivers flow)
I seldom bothered the shutters to shut,
for the northern maids are the warmingest, O.

But when I came on to the company town
(at a waterwheel pinch the rivers flow)
I hastened to pull the shades all down,
for the midland maids are the harmingest, O.

But when I moved down to the shore of the sea
(at a waterwheel pinch the rivers flow)
I threw the doors open fancy and free,
for the southern maids are the charmingest, O.

## ARIADNE ABANDONED

My heart is blowing through the wind—
O what a bitter blow!
The three ragged witches blown off the sea
cry, "Tear up the world! All love must go!"

## LOONY TOM'S SONG

Give me a tune and I'll slap the bull fife,
I'll spring the hornblower out of his wife.

Any old flutist you care to uncover,
give me his name and I'll be her lover.

  La diddle la, the hydrant chatted.
  Um titty um, the milkpail said.

For love hid the story under the songbook,
buried the ballad under the hornbook.

Love so they tell me, love so I hear,
love waves the trumpet and butters the tree.

But love will come tooting only if free.
And only to me.

  La diddle la, the hydrant chatted.
  Um titty um, the milkpail said.

## ELEGY OF THE QUEEN OF SHEBA

What golden glory can the eunuchs promise
to sing me back to any dance of praise?
Never shall summer come to Babylon again
a sunbursting Eden of naked days.
*O heavy heart, my heavy longing,*
*heaviness all heart, and the apricots falling!*

Only baboons are left prancing round me,
left beating time to the littered glory—
where I have no song, no sunstruck dance,
no peril to lilt my story.
*O heavy heart, my heavy longing,*
*heaviness all heart, and the apricots falling!*

## THE PASSIONATE PEACEMAKER TO HIS LOVE

Very well: you may bring back your portable hammer,
your scathing needlework, and the monkey wrench too.
I relent, and though I keep a rueful humor,
behold the olive branches in the double room.

However: terms of hospitality are much more stern.
This time your bloodhound must stay out of my closet,
cats kept in their bag, both our goats getting turns,
and for restabling your high horse an upkeep deposit.

So then: you may unpack your gun-powder talcum,
your driftwood nightgown and your garden-party tools.
I repent, although I keep in my rueful welcome
a graduate diploma from your wrestling school.

## SCHERZO FOR THREE MAIDEN LADIES

Hoo hoo, Miss Addie! Do you know where they went?
  Who?
The waltzer, the whistler, and the candyman.
  He was here a shake ago.
    And so were they.
O lord, Miss Bessie, now who will pay the rent?

Was it when the Bishop phoned that they ran away?
  Who?
The cycler, the tootler, and the handyman.
  He was here a jump ago.
    And so were they.
Why are men always running off to try another sport?

  Well men you know—
    Men, O!
  You never know with them.
    No!
They're always running off to try another sport.
  Hell! Men, you know—
    Men, O!
  You never know with them!
    No!
What a shame when life is long that men are growing short.

O lord, Miss Carrie, will they ever come back?
  Who?
The waltzer! The whistler! The candyman!
  Oh Oh! Boo hoo, boo hoo!
    God damn!
The cycler and the tootler and the handy handyman!

# *Winter is a Widow*

## THE WIFE OF REMARKABLE SAM

O where did the sun go down with my heart?
Once all mornings beamed on me at my front door.
I swept on roller skates around the kitchen floor
when I was a pretty bride and loved my Sam.

From Niagara on his motorbike he brought me home
to our housing-project heaven behind the baseball park.
And I could hardly wait till each day turned dark
to feel him around me, to feel my Sam.

But one day the sun went down with my heart.
O where's the fairest steeplejack of Chesapeake Bay?
Here upon his tombstone I lie and lackaday
of when I was a pretty bride and loved my Sam.

## THE AGING BALLETOMANE

Once I had wild geese to keep my flying—
no creaking toes nor needled eyes
like these in the now rain sighing.
    O ago so long, alas!

Fleetly in bird shoes I led and I leapt
(my raven girl whirling a red-cloud skirt)
and there were no mists where I wept.
    O in the days when we danced!

Shall my feet now rust in a barnyard rain?
Or might by chance one last high goose
come flying this chase again?
    O ago so long, how it passed!

## DON GIOVANNI TO THE VERY NICE NEW VIRGIN

Is there something dull about the innocent?
That your simple glowing is a glow too pure, and an irritant?

Were I a reforming pagan or Blake's holy child
I might come to you to play at angels incorruptible,
in the childhood of a world set its age aside
and embrace a maid demure with dulcet mood inviolable.

But I am too bedeviled by grand old jigs of Lucifer
to relish minuets Goody-Two-Shoed and petite:
though the world looks dancing candy to the green-armed amateur,
I, a Peter Pan unlikely, now prefer more bitter sweets.

So, despite your simple glowing both adorable and innocent,
purity that bores is strictly God's divertissement.

## NOCTURNE OF MADAME BOVARY

When the night is dead black and the pillow hard
the question of one's longing shivers in the air.
What can I answer it? What dare I whisper?
I am wed to cold Leontes, the owner of my bed.
Snow sifts between us a skeleton shroud.
*Half the bed is hot, the other half cold,*
*colder is the bed of my old moon.*

The forest fires of summer are a ghostly grove.
Who did not love enough? Who will not give?
I lie in a bed beside the North Pole—
the master of my night is a polar bear of stone.
Chill chamber! what a sleepless heart I hold
toward the dying fire of all that I remember.
*Half the bed is hot, the other half cold,*
*colder is the bed of my old moon.*

## THE HIGHLAND PIPER'S TUNE

Can you still run a race with a maiden,
old man McTortoise?
Still take the quick trick with a flounce, Mac,
as ready as any young man?

Though bouncey a mile one minx may sprint
there'll be many a drizzly day to trot,
for it's long far long to the monuments.
And where shall you be without a true love,
or how shall you go with no love of your own
along the long road to the pearly tent
where the final amusements begin?

Or will you not get there, old Mac my man?

## THE GOODNIGHT DREAM OF BUFFALO BILL

As far far up as any holy truth can fly
I will toss my best cap, my saddle and spur,
up upon the blue meadow where wild angels roam
I will unrope my heart and lasso the sky.
It's way out in that open, above time and weather,
I shall find us the perch of a model high home,
for there roosts the dream I am meaning to live
in the wondrous wide bed on the lap of God.
    Love is a red-letter bird, my dear,
    Love is a red-letter bird.

Then good luck and goodbye to cold swans in the bush,
for till judgments add up and all kingdoms come
the hope of the heavenly wing boils down
to the dove that nests handy and hot to the touch.
So come, let's light out with the sun and the moon
for our long after-life up in Paradise Town
in the dream that I dream I am meaning to live
on the wondrous wide bed in the lap of God.
    Love is a four-letter word, my dear,
    Love is a four-letter word.

V

# *True & False Unicorn*

*A Tapestry of Voices*

FOR KERMIT SHEETS

*Canst thou bind the unicorn with his band in the furrow? or will he harrow the valleys after thee? Wilt thou trust him because his strength is great? or wilt thou leave thy labour to him? Wilt thou believe him, that he will bring home thy seed, and gather it into thy barn?*
—JOB

*Commonly it dangles down like a turkey-cock's comb, but when a unicorn has a mind to fight or put it to any other use, what does he do but make it stand, and then it is as straight as an arrow.*
—RABELAIS

*13-1/2% Alcohol (used solely as a solvent and preservative), Vitamin B1 (Thiamin), Black Cohosh, Pleurisy Root, Life Root Plant, Chamomile, Dandelion, Licorice, Jamaica Dogwood (Piscidia Erythrina), True and False Unicorn, Gentian.*
—advertised contents of Lydia E. Pinkham's Vegetable Compound

## I. BEFORE THE ARRAS

*(The Unicorn questions the nature of the chase.)*

THE LION, *Reading:*
In China the unicorn is King of Beasts.
On the uplands of Utopia his nest is found.
He occupies an office in the sacred wood.
Despite his delicacy he is indestructible.
He defends with his life the Cinderella kingdoms.
He donates his blood to the Holy Ghost.
Once he worsted the elephant in combat
(reported St. Isidore who was at the scene)
and merely his presence intimidates Behemoth.
Often in summer he unrobes the new moon.
And between Orion and the Major Dog
his stars are the semen of the Milky Way.

SIGMUND OF VIENNA:
Unnatural beasts abide in every natural history.
In the anatomy of Unreason man's nature thrives.
We all are hunters of the unicorn.
Heaven's bestiary holds a quarry uncatalogued.
To ravish the fabulous is our secret prayer.
We all are hunters of the unicorn.
And if we should trap him, would he verify our dreams?
Or would we be saddled with his own bête noire?
We all are hunters of the unicorn.
And the unicorn hunts for himself.

THE UNICORN:
I am the unicorn, but is that I?
What is the unicorn? Who am I?

Am I more unreal than a flying fish?
Am I more animal than I could wish?

Whether my passions be mock or real,
how shall I know till I see what I feel?

If I am fantasy, I am also its flesh.
Am I less real than my own anguish?

Whether my feelings be false or true,
how can I say till I see what I do?

What is a unicorn? And is that I?
I am the unicorn. But who am I?

TOM FOOL:
Identities are mixed by Mother Moon
    in a trefoil vat
    of this and that
mixed with a great horn spoon.

Grand Daddy Sun hangs them out to dry
    roaring Who is who?
    Are you one or two?
hangs them out in their incubi.

SIGMUND OF VIENNA:
In the nature of things there is usually a question,
in the vision of things unusually an answer.
    We all are hunters of the unicorn.
Does the taxidermist ever behold the live beast?
Did the marksman crack the mirror in the jungle?
    The unicorn hunts for himself.

## II. HORN AND HOUNDS

*(Entering the wilderness the Unicorn is beset by voices.)*

YOUNG SAGITTARIUS:
In the misty land where the unicorns grow
in a forest of nubile plums they grow,
frisky stallions under juicy trees
they grow they grow and their horns do grow
as they thrust and dally and prance the ground
through orchards of plums in green,
in the misty land where horns abound
in the land where the unicorns grow.

A VIRGIN, *Waiting:*
He will have a long horn on his brow,
the legs of a horse, an antelope's throat
the tail of a lion, the beard of a goat
　　(and the child of my loins is desire
　　the child in my loins is on fire)
he will have a long horn on his brow,
O the long unique horn on his brow!

From the unbridled circus of dream
trotting bareback round my dark
he comes the pure wish of my fear.
His head in my lap, O, lie down!
　　(and the child of my loins is desire)
This prince unclothed by a crone,
will I fetter or free his spell?
Am I sweet enough bait for his crown
or do I smell strong of my fear?
　　(the child in my loins is on fire)

O, his head in my lap, lie down!
His head in my lap, O the crown!

THE EMPRESS OF BYZANTIUM:
To the Indies, to Thule, dispatch nets!
Marshal the Amazons, prepare a crusade.
Fetch me the exorbitant horn.

Deflower all nymphs, martyr all nuns,
pay the witch in the wood any price!
For that male cornucopia I thirst.

Without great folly life is a death.
I will grasp, I will drink up man's mystery.
Poison or not, it is Love.

QUEEN VICTORIA:
O pretty pony, naughty pet,
    you pale poetic chap,
you stay out late at night too much
    without a proper wrap.
Come live with me a neater life
    secure from all mishap.

For pleasant walks you've ample lawn,
    for naps a velvet bed,
and if you nicely wag your tail
    there's extra gingerbread,
while tartan bows will much enhance
    that thing upon your head.

If you're to be a gentleman
and not a little pest,
quips and pranks and running wild
had better be suppressed.
Remember, God and Mother know
exactly what is best.

HIS HONOR THE MAYOR:
A highbrow jackass is what you are,
more trouble than you're worth.
No home no job no security card
no certificate of birth.
You're a highly suspicious joke.

We don't want exotic vagrants here
causing some queer disgrace.
All the stags in this town are clean he-men
proud to be commonplace.
You're very much too baroque.

Go back where you came from, shake a leg,
the hell with your fairy tale.
If there's any more horny monkeyshines
we'll straighten you out in jail.
You're a menace to decent folk.

EUROPA, *Weeping:*
Deliver me from desuetude, O unicorn, return to us!
Bring back my Aquitaine. Recall my cavaliers.
I am damp, I am dwindling in the hampers of the lame.
They would launder me away with the fogs of dread.

Herald home my troubadours, O four-legged horn!
Smothered are the infants of merriment here.
Worry turns me rabbit-witted, tedious for ten.
And mould collects faster than the larks arrive.

Unbutton, Tristan, this rut I am belted to.
Leave me unlocked and freshly looked out for.
Merlin, Merlin, I am rotting for a rape!
My armadillos are in heat, they unnerve me.

Rescue me, my paladin, repitch my rained-out camp.
Resurrect the garlands of liveliness once lived.
Revive and run again for my gauntlet of grace.
If my lead foot offends thee, break it off!

O unicorn, recaper! Bring knighthood to reflower!
Abduct me, wed me, re-renaissance my life!
Else Doom will take me in his cold wet arms,
Doom will seduce me in a drowning bed.

BIG BLACK SAMBO:
Look down, sweet Unicorn, come down my Savior,
I is lookin for to gallop you Home.
When I gets to Heaven gonna shine up my Lord,
gonna ride my Lord all around, O Lord,
gonna win every Holy Derby.
Man, there's honey in that horn for me!

When he shake his head, he jar the river,
when he gets runnin, he crack the mountain,
he's the purebred thoroughbred unicorn of God.
They got nothin like him roamin wild in Texas,

they got nothin like him in a millionaire's garage.
He's the speediest highest class Savior on record.
O blue-ribbon favorite, Lord, give me a lift!

I been huntin everywheres for you, White Savior,
I wants to be your jockey, I wants to be your groom.
Got strong black arms for any whitewashin needs
like sweepin after angels or movin round clouds.
Though I is black as the Congo, I aint no devil,
I just needin that good job, Lord, with you.
Lemme clean out your stable the rest of my days!

O white beauty champion, lemme hitch a ride
and give em all somethin to gawk at fine.
My midnight body on your pearly bareback,
me holdin your horn for all my dear life,
let's us go out huntin *them* for a change
all around the U.S. all around the atlas,
right up to the President's white front door,
and watch me spit in his eye!

Raise me up, glory winner, you is my Savior,
I is lookin for to gallop you Home.
When I gets to Heaven gonna polish that horn,
gonna ride my Lord all around, O Lord,
gonna win the apocalypse all hands down.
Brother, get a load of that grail!

## III. SNARE AND DELUSION

*(In the heart of the desert the silence is piercing.)*

THE UNICORN, *Wounded:*
Of whose fantasy am I prisoner?
Whose animal, real or unreal?
I am their unicorn, but who is he?

In nocturnal shrines they would lock me up
or else trick me into their trim corrals
as servitor, scion, and family ghost.

Do I reasonably belong to these petit-point realms
more than to my own unreasonable?
I am their unicorn, he is not I.

Monarchs have sold off my private forest,
merchants have corrupted my alchemy.
The atavistic cost of being avatar!

I, dispossessed and unpossessable,
alien anomaly at the suburbs' edge,
I too endure hunger and doubt and cold.

And how shall I conceal my nakedness here?—
white, like a maiden's moonlit belly,
white, like an undressed Absolute.

White is the final pure negation:
sterile gown of the hospital room,
winding sheet, skeleton, the ash.

Animate and inanimate, O ambiguous steed!
In Jabberwock land, or Elysium—
where am I truly or falsely at home?

I am the charm sought for a miracle,
I am the harm mocked for a failure.
I am both savior and scapegoat.

Who is my unicorn, and am I he?

On my head this heavy cockade I bear.
Stigma? Trumpery? Benison? Diadem?
How to make feather of mad handicap?

Not ram or bull, not Pan or Lucifer,
I wear this pale celibate tusk,
a horn without twin or progeny.

From a bastard mare's-nest I sprang,
hybrid of the horn-rimmed Gothick.
I am my unicorn, he is not mine.

What hope have I in the open veldt
with antler, billygoat, or rhinoceros?
My guilt sits exposed on my brow.

A touch-and-go glory, this decorator's spear!
Honest animal-lovers at the carnival
hesitate to bless or abuse it.

And how shall I mate? Who is my love?
I have wearied my reflection in the well.
He is my unique-horn, I am not he.

O shame shame of the shocking singular!
Am I merely some fragile lost absurd,
a eunuch's beautiful monster-child,

brideless, anonymous of brood,
hamstrung by a magnificent fallacy?
I am my unicorn, but who am I?

For in natural history's joke I stay writ,
admired malaprop of the bestial book.
Huntsman, carry me home for a Snark!

On the horns of my legend, alas, am I hoist:
how can my inconceivable self
marry its joy and its scorn?

I am my unicorn, he is not I.

## IV. "MON SEUL DÉSIR"

*(The Unicorn reaches a temple in a clearing.)*

SIGMUND OF VIENNA:
Lucidities of the Past develop labyrinths.
Enigmas of the Present await their focus.
The singular riddle blurs the self-portrait
double exposed to curse and blessing.
Accept the mixture cracked in the mirror.
Absolute clarity is the mystery beyond.

TOM FOOL:
Hosanna to the odd bird much maligned,
    queer fish, fool,
    exception to the rule—
Glory be to God for the one of a kind!
Horray for prodigy, fluke, and freak.
    Nonesuch, hail,
    eccentrically prevail—
Hallelujah for the living thing unique!

THE LION:
Monocerous mystery, you are no man's gazelle,
you are your own and your angel's fox,
quest of the wild, fillip of the tame
on the trail of mercurial paradox.
    You shall outwit and outlive the hounds.

You collect talismans behind the Sun's back.
The Moon signs your metamorphic sleep
with owl, with moth, and with nightingale,
star on the mountain, crescent in the deep.
    You shall outwit and outlive the hounds.

You know the webworking trick of the spider,
the serpent's grasp on the bough of life.
Yours is a changeling flesh to espouse
for your soul has bedded a magic wife.
    You shall outwit and outlive the hounds.

Mascot loyal to the three-faced Muse,
you are the poet's hermaphrodite.
Echo and song and their incantation,
you foretell wisdom and love in the night.
    You shall outwit and outlive the hounds.

THE UNICORN:
    Lion Lion, burning gold,
    burn hot, burn bold,
        burn burn
        O Coeur de Leon
    burn bright my flickering cold.

O lustrous Leo, thou art my sunburst.
Give me each day thy daily delight.
Hold me and heat me, thou art my steadfast,
topaz guide to my quicksilver flight.

O gentle, O genital, my golden Leo,
heal and garden my moonstruck scourge.
Apollinate the fallow, sweat me into flower,
fireball fertile of my Demiurge.

Ripen me, Leo, my honeyhive and root,
fecundating bonfire, thou art my need.
Succulent harvest, fruit of the Lion,
O shower me in golden seed.

        Lion Lion, burning gold,
        burn hot, burn bold,
                burn burn
                O fleur de Leo
        burn bright my irresolute cold.

TOM FOOL:
Through the glaring haze of Time
        Sun and Moon
        go in and out
        go round and over
        in naked pursuit
forever lighting their lights
        halo flame
        penumbra glow
        in shameless love
        go up and down
through the truculent gaze of Time
        brazenly one
        incendiary two
        fireworking death
        revive reignite
forever cohabiting light
through the fair and foul race
        of time being
        time after time
through the gloating rape of Time.

THE VIRGIN'S LULLABY:
Sweet desire has lived its dream,
lull lull and rock, my heart,
hammock happy in my breast.

All desire now sweet and clean,
washed away, in pleasure washed,
my desire has gone to rest.

Sweet sweet sweet desire,
sleep fair, rock your nest,
dream again of when you rise
    again again
    for beauty's eyes.

SIGMUND OF VIENNA:
In shooting gallery, or Deluge, or zoo of the saints
unnatural beasts assert their natural virtue.
    We all are hunters of the unicorn.
His grace is whelped from the ogre of heartache.
His coronation sweats in the palace of wisdom.
    We all are hunters of the unicorn.
In spite of the questions that raise a question
the treasure of his brow will shine in the asking.
    The unicorn hunts for us all.

THE UNICORN:
So, O my burden, art thou my bride?
My dark, my gold? My new, my old?
Then ride me out of history, ride me through fact,
ride me to the marriage of heaven and hell.
And if we are welcome in the peaceable kingdom
I will pasture my vitals by the cabala tree
with my Lion's heart at the root
my horn in the sap of Love
breathing new blood into wilder game
for the reforestations of poetry.

This is my only, this is my fate.
This is my godhead grown from doubt.
I am my unicorn, and he is I.

I am myself my own true and false.
I am myself my real unreal.
He is my unicorn, and I am he.

This is my I, my one, my me.
This is my own, my two, my we.
I am my unicorn, and so is he.

VI

# *Whistling in the Labyrinth*

DEDICATED TO
HELEN ADAM, JESS COLLINS, ROBERT DUNCAN,
MADELINE GLEASON AND EVE TRIEM
IN MEMORY OF THE MAIDEN.

# *Rubrics*

## UNDER THE HANGED MAN'S TREE

Black, white, yellowing, and red,
all will be well to fall
under the apple greenwood
under the green apple tree.

> *Mrs Pharisey wishes a picnic*
> *but the ground is too wet to sit out.*
> *Tell her Osiris is dead.*

Black, white, yellowing to red,
all will be well in falling
to swim in the deepest corners
to float on the restless well.

> *She would laugh at him upside down*
> *under the greenwood apple*
> *standing in the muck on his head.*

But he will be well in all
black, white, yellowing, or red.
The blood will rise from the roots,
the fruit will fall from the wounds.

> *Any picnic under this tree*
> *suits better her harvesting daughter*
> *who relishes wine and bread.*

## SERMON OF THE HOLY INFANT

I am born I am born at the dying of the year
    down from the Dove up from the Dark
    out to the Light of My Lady's lap
where the birth and the death and the life are one
    and the first word I speak is Love.

O wintry children in your Age of Fire,
burning blood-freezing sacrifices
on thunderbolt toys lit with cold blood,
will you gladly assassinate my Unicorn
to enthrone Rhinoceros lord of the world
in blind thunder—the boomerang beast
who rules in rage, who reaps in dust
the wormwood jungle in the heart of man?

When your brothers are burnt to bleeding trees,
your Father's earth burnt to sands of bone,
when, turning to grief what was born for joy,
you hurl your Hell-flood cloud of Cain
down upon my Mother and me,
will you kneel in praise where a Harpy's claw
dandles the shriveling idiot babe
who announces your hope of the world?

I am born I am born at the dying of the year
    down from the Dove up from the Dark
    out to the Light of My Lady's lap
where the birth and the death and the life are one
    and the last word I speak is Love.

## MY APE MY LAMB

Ape in my ribcage, Ape my sin,
locked in the captive flesh I wear,
Anthropoidos of my labyrinth
hugs my bones in stubborn embrace.

Sin-fat Ape, the grunt in my breast,
who gulped my hive, who raped my bird,
Ape of the mirror within the mirror
bangs on my walls for another kiss.

As I try to climb the circular stairs,
to climb beyond my crucified chambers,
dragging uphill his beastly devotion
limps my hope in a hairy cape.

Listen to my Apecage: Feed me! he howls,
I have lapped up your Lady, lopped your Father.
Now nibble I you afoul in my maw!
Leaden together let us wallow down!

* * *

Hobbling at carnival, astray, I beheld
a fleece newborn to clothe my coping,
to heat my lack, to gold my giving—
lost by the fairgrounds I found the Lamb.

Frisky in white that infant mascot
followed me home, follows me still
to turn the page of my wedding hymn—
but Ape, old Ape, has soiled that gown!

Around the towerings of my spiral stair,
too laden to climb or stand upright
with Ape on my heart and Lamb on my heel
I stagger under the unmated weight.

Keeper of cage and shepherd untended,
I am eaten inside, I am hungered out.
O Lamb, loyal Lamb! When wilt thou grow,
O Lamb, to devour the Ape in me?

## THE BLUE FLOOD-TREE

It began with the smallest leaves.
I had been trying to determine
the shape of stem and branch
in the way the old woman demanded,
she who was vexed by my fumble.

Until suddenly I saw for myself
the true color of her ancient tree.
They are blue, I said, look!
they are lapis leaves.
Of course, you dummkopf! said she.

Each leaf had yet another blue leaf
all growing on the Blue Flood-Tree
which contained the original waters.
And the delta that opened to the roots
flowed down through my very own veins.

What else did you expect? said the old woman.

## BIRTHDAY POEM

Birth. Day.
My day of birth. My birth of days?
But any day or every day awakes a birth
and meets a death.
And every day Old I and New I
collide and crash in Me.

There have been many Novembers
long and short living with I.
All one's life this life with I,
much too long and far too short:
for better or worse, for richer or purer,
in sickness in health, till life do us part,
till resurrection may possibly
make us One.

Dear old
hot and cold, recalcitrant and bold Mr. I—
with one eye looking out and one eye looking in—
do not forget your spectacles.
The Light of Heaven dwells in the 3rd eye
at the root of the unicorn's horn.
And what do you see from there?

O dear 3rd the Other,
bring this day the telegram from Anima Mundi
with some light for the mirror of wisdom.
We await every day her illuminating summons,
the identity card written clear out:

when Old I and New I take hand in hand
  take heart, take forth
    serenely riding to God O
    with only One I in mind.

## REBIRTHDAY CARD

How did you first set forth
and what is the final step?
Having rounded the multiples
and arrived at one,
do you think it especially
a flat-footing route
if both eyes are open
and the tailbone straight?

Throughout the mountain runs
thickness of granite
while under whale-spout
sinks a swallowing tunnel.
Go on! Coming up to morning
finding the roads blocked
Sun re-erects a highway
to the rising above.

Ah ripening gold,
to come to fruition where
these coins count!
The Murphys next door have
strangled in their loopholes.
Blind Mr. Stone on the corner
says, 'Is it time to cross?
What does the light say?'

## STANDING IN THE NEED

Standing in the need of<br>
      lark on the lamppost<br>
      furniture in the valley—<br>
coming along under the trees I<br>
had a hard time keeping<br>
my head clear.<br>
      Them branches!<br>
      from scratch . . .<br>
And crossing over the river<br>
I had a moment of<br>
      madness<br>
            in the mud.

Ah to be seeing it   seen<br>
      like this most<br>
unlikely opening   open!<br>
      From the pot of . . .<br>
      and the particles<br>
the whole two-sided birth of a<br>
      building<br>
      (in and out)<br>
erected between parentheses.<br>
Too it will be time to<br>
      speak it soon.

Already<br>
            ark! ark!<br>
my puppy dog barks in<br>
      the basement<br>
hearing far off<br>
                    a key.

Then
when I open the door of the
    sweet common place
will a child leap forth
                with a toy?

## THE OLD GUITARIST UNDER THE FREEWAY

I am homesick for a land I have never seen,
  sang the old guitarist under the freeway.
A place to be pleased with simple pleasures
is the hideaway hope of the daily dribbler.
What will bustle and indolence ever make dear?

I am homesick for a land I have never seen,
  sang the lone guitarist under the freeway.
How do we measure what horizon we want
when the wanting is made of old bedding down?
Is it yet another wandering back to here?

I am homesick for a land I have never seen,
  sang the cold guitarist under the freeway.
I want to be going every place in the world
but I don't want to budge from right now.
O hard-to-please fidgeter, where is my there?

All lands are the one land where you are,
  replied the guitar string under his hand.
Be more content, my plucking flower.
What is here is everywhere elsewhere,
what is not here is nowhere at all,
  sang the old guitar string under the freeway.

## THE GIFT OF THE STAG

At the cold extremity of that November night
sudden sunflowers budded from the stone beach
where I lay dismantled there on the shore
victim of my lost faun's fate.

At the extreme of my despair on that cold night
flickering down the thicket slope lightly leaping
came the stag a white stag descending to the cove—
the old Wapiti Chief leaping down to driftwood.

Bold of antennae, lord of all wave lengths,
he drank the moonwind off kelp and foam,
he devoured the shadows under shell and stone
before he came inquiring to my feet.

Hail, Elk King! I cried, Hail, Forest Lord!
Forgive me that I cannot rise to honor thee.
Drowned by my sorrows I lie shipwrecked here
too crippled to crawl to my knees.

Three times the great stag circled where I lay,
three times pawed away the wet stones round my brow,
then silently kneeling beside my fatal wound
he laid his crown in my hands.

And all the pebbles were petaled where I stood.

## A LITURGY FOR POETS

PREPARATION

Orpheus be with thee.
And with thy spirit.

In thought, word, and deed
arise, enter, and aroint
early early
before the scavengers arrive.
On rusted edges of old abuses,
dead motors of burned-out hells
stand ready steady
to hoist to hurl
into the pit with pick and choose
your thought, word, and deed.

Orpheus be with thee.
And with high spirit.
Let us array.

PETITION

Kneel down in the draft
and hail to her, eight times hail
St. Sally of Forth, Holy Sempstress,
who sits in the crypt sewing, saying,
'It all shall come stitch-up
if thumb's in the thimble,'
nods as her needle works
down and up of in and out
cross, patch, cross.

Hearken unto her teaching:
    Unbucket! Avaunt!
    Unbuckle the wraparounds!
    Unclock the well-fit cloak!
    There is more in the pinnings than pins.

    Cut the umbilical
    but hold the thread.
    Untwine unwind the wounded and wound-up.
    Thou shalt not ravel in a duckout!

    De-wart! Enhance!
    Or Glory goes forward
    no more than a pace,
    keeps its turnabout uppermost.
Here endeth a first lesson of many.

Kneel untrousered in the draft
and hail fair Sally of Forth and Far,
St Sally Clotho, Virgin Tailor,
who sews together lowly pants
for the long highroad occasions.

CREDO: THE THREE TRINITIES
I believe in the Three Appearances of
the Beast to be Loved
as our Lord of Unmercy has taught us:
    *Uno,* full-faced snout,
    nose behind noose,
    golden of lips
    and crowning mitre,
    *Due,* muscular torso

under buttons and belts,
expandable trunk
and hearth of guts.
*Tre,* lurk-behinder,
the comet's tail,
self-winding spouter
on goat-legged dance.
From these three together grows
the One as the Fourth
that must be obeyed.

And I believe in the Three Faces of
Shibella Gloria, daughter of Glorious Shiva,
whose initial face proclaims:
Attain the inevitable!
Whose double face announces:
The temple of the home is
not the center of the world,
outside there's a bigger squeeze.
The temple of the world
will take you back home
when you learn to walk on your knees.
Whose third face, O, is
the mystery of four,
explains all other faces.
When she takes off her glasses
prepare for the blinding jolt.

If I falter in these,
if I fail to believe,
I must needs turn back and
perform the Three Disappointments:

*A*, as in Youth—
the natural lean of the head
leading neatly to atrophy.
*B*, as in Middle Man—
the lift of the sword in arm
leading to decay.
*C*, as in Final Snake—
where atrophy meets decay
and the skin is shed
yea, it is shed
but all it contained as well.

ORDINATION

Scribbler communicant, hopeful drum-major,
will you abide by the pilgrimage,
will you honor the itinerary?
You must go over the Paps of Mummy,
you must go under the Behaving Well,
you must go round the Marry Mire,
you must go past the Mighthave Bin.

Lord Shakespeare, I am unworthy!

Are you resolved to meet your making?
Are you eager to
be chewed by dragon teeth,
swallowed by whaledam,
spit from lion's mouth?
Are you zealous
to die for your divining rod?

Apollo, have mercy upon me!

Babblebard dreamer, would-be savior,
when you have asked the name of the Nameless,
when you have heard the Voice in the Wall,
when you have hunted the unfettered Opposites
still roaming wild in chaos,
will you bring back to us whatever
flower you find in the stone?

Hail Great Mother, aid my song!
Pray for my death in the birth of now!

# *Visitations*

## THE NIGHT WATCH OF THE MAGDALENE

On the long outskirts of a dismantled city
    toward the final flicker of dusk
I entered the nave of an unfinished cathedral
and found Mary Magdalene cooking up a stew,
the stove a glow as red as her hair
and a three-forked spoon in her hand.

Dear lady, my feet ache, I said to her,
I've come all the way from my Dad's hometown
    trying to find his footsteps.

Have a sip of my chowder, sir, said she,
I've been stirring and poking this pot for years,
it won't cure all, nor is it lethal,
it's rich in folly and savors of rue
but it sometimes helps in the middle of the night.

Well, there comes a time when you just don't care any more.
So I took a taste, and another, and again.
Isn't it tangy? said she, the receipt is direct
    from my Aunt Pandora.
But I with the third spoon undammed at the ducts
a salt drench enough to drown us both.

Alack, said she, one remedy always requires another.
Can you look through the tears to the stars in the eye?
      I squinted and peered,
I hadn't seen a star for a year and a half,
and in this wet focus all I saw
was a full baby moon splash over the altar.

Perhaps, said Magdalene, it's high your time
to take a turn on our Great Roundabout
      out in the Virgin's wing.
And she led me outside by an inside door
behind the graves, between the dogs
and brought me to a field where above us rose
      encompassing the cold black sky
the interlacy circle of a ferris-looking Wheel
as gigantic as a grounded planet.

Hop aboard, my boy, we'll get things moving—
that is, if I can figure what switch to throw
that makes the damn thing work. I'm not the
regular operator, though I never forget a number.

She cranked a huge key, and without a sound
      lifted me into the night
on a dangling swivel-seat built for two
      where I hung on tight alone.
Have a good time, there's plenty to go around!
and she scurried down cellar to pump the juice,
while up the ascending arc I floated
      ascending the dark
on that vast slow-moving Wheel.

Then I noticed there were other riders aboard
who had been going round on a regular basis
    night after night
    year after year:
there were figureheads and maidenhoods,
goddesses, martyrs, and washerwomen,
Nuestra Senora de Guadalupe,
Sappho, Delilah, and Mother Goose
    all silently rotating there.
And each must have drunk from Magdalene's kettle
for the darkness was wet with salty rain.

By the time midnight struck I was soaked to a shiver
    and barely halfway aloft.
Old witch! I called down.
Why did you hang me up here in the dark
with all these great big girls?

    A megaphone lit up far below
    and Magdalene's laughter came rocketing back:
It's only in the dark that the Light can circulate,
it's only in the dark that one can witness
    the truly extinguishing Light!

But where, I cried, is this
wheel of misfortune going?

Don't worry, she answered, it works its way round.
The Fathers and Sons are on the other side
and it all comes together in the end. Good night!
I'll be back in the morning with breakfast, although
you may likely come down in a different country.

And her lamp went out
and the wind came up
and tears dripped down
and the dark spread wider and wider arms
as I,
miniature dial on that enormously numberless clock,
rose higher around the night.

## GAVIN AND THE GREEN UNCLE

At break of day on the first of October
my ancient Uncle roused me from bed,
my beknighted Green Uncle knocked at my cottage
and asked me for my head.

Since he lives in the city in a basement apartment
and travels all the year through,
I see him only on serious occasions,
for he is my godfather too.

Said he, as he took an axe from his satchel,
Did you hear the last cockcrow?
Kneel down! Kneel down, my sluggish nephew,
and pay me the debt you owe!

But why, I said, this premature payment?
My year is not up till Christmas Day
when I'm sworn to bring you my total income.
Why reckon it today?

Your Father is sorely grieved by your thinking,
said my Uncle, honing his blade.

He wants the disorder removed completely
    before it grows more decayed.

Does he think, said I, my effort is finished?
    I have worlds yet to see and to hear.
Take him my heartache or my agile fingers!
    But my head is still unclear.

Precisely! said Uncle, Let's get down to business!
    Sighing, I bent my knee
and pled my last Hail to the Holy Mother
    as I heard him count up to three.

With a masterful stroke my neck he severed,
    my head rolled off at the whack.
But I crawled along after it over the carpet
    and carefully put it back.

Well done! cried Uncle, does it now fit better?
    I had to admit this was so.
Then I went and fetched my old scout hatchet
    and dealt him blow for blow.

Though the strike ricocheted, my knife had dented
    his hoary green wound a rip.
Yet he rose, embraced me, adjusted his collar
    and packed off for another trip.

Wait, Uncle! Take back this shrunken girdle
    you gave me when I was born.
For my final autumn I will rise up unbelted
    as naked as this morn,

and my head I shall bring as a gift of crystal
  when I greet you on Christmas Day . . .
That remains to be seen! God help you, my boy!
  he called back as he rode away.

## THREE VISITS TO THE VIRGIN

When I dared my first leap up to her nimbus
I saw her tender sapphires fill with tears,
her cheek a rosarium, rosemary her hair
with a new moon the comb in her sturdy fingers.
I nestled for an hour in that uplifting lap
where she crooned Halloo-i-ay and murmured to me:
One in 2000 is one in a million too
leaving many an infant yet to be borne,
so turn yourself over and I'll clean you off
to see what we find when we get to the bottom.
If you know what the end is, you can make a start.
  After my bath she told me to come back tomorrow
  and she handed me down to her sphinxes
  the sphinxes knitting in the bulrushes
  who didn't have much to say.

Thus my second high-jump was scarcely prepared
to land in the arms of a Big Black Mammy
humming holy redhot and tapping out the blues.
She laughed when I took her for Our Lady's maid:
I'm the Madmadmadam of this old mansion,
I been working my way up since I was a kid.
Can't you tell, chile, from the number out front?
It once was un-numerable, it's now 3 in 1,
and as values go up, they can open a penthouse.

If Glory, boy, pushes the right elevator button
together maybe we'll all assumpt!
  When she'd polished my digits and put me down
  the sphinxes still sat among the storks
  the long-faced sphinxes sat there knitting
  and they had even less to say.

On my next upswing to that big armchair there
with a nose bifocaled sat white-haired Sophia
lullabyeing a polyphonic Rockabye of Ages.
I, she said, am your great grand very good Mother,
I've been mothering so long I've grown three breasts
and their names are: Always, Mary, and Bright.
So I'll tell you a thoughtful bedtime story.
Once upon a time lived happily ever after
because he discovered which mouth to feed.
Now here's a crumb, here's a drop of wine.
If you absorb them, come back to stay.
  When she set me down the sphinxes gaped
  the sphinxes stopped knitting and dropped their jaws
  and they all said: Oo! Ah! Alley Oop Eluia!
  As it was in the beginning it's apt to continue!

## A VISIT FROM THREE MUSES

I was out in the chicken yard, minding the hencoop,
sitting there hard on my daily predicament—
can you hatch a new songbird from a tired old nest?—
and having on the whole a rather uninspiring time,
when lo and behold me, three tall women came
dancing through the chicken yard
right across the chicken mash!
Three peachier graces you never saw painted.

Now I'm a simple type fellow, with complicated dreams.
I've had a lot of visions and met some grand people.
But these unexpected visitors were as real as a clock.

My name is Fay Morgan, said the one in gold.
My name is Kitty Hawk, said the one in blue.
My name is Ruby Hill, said the one in red.
We're your three muses, they said in unison,
and we've come to be amused.

Well, I stood on my head and blew my rusty trumpet.
I tried an old cantata but I'd lost my pitch-pipe.
I'm sorry, girls, said I, things haven't been moving.
All I have is a predicament that's unpredictable.

You deserve a better fate, said They.
Of course, but what is it? said I.
We're It! said the Three.

Who works it? said I.
You do, said Ruby.
With me, said Kitty.
With us! said Fay.
Then you're hired, said I.

Fay Morgan clamped a vibrator to my head.
Kitty Hawk drove a corkscrew into my heart.
Ruby Hill made certain my genitals were on,
then she tickled the soles of my feet.

Light foot it! said she.
Light heart it! said Kitty.

Light head it! said Fay.
Illuminations! quoth I.
And we did a quick quadrille, right between the hens.

What keeps it moving? said I.
Keeping it in motion, said They.
Move things around! Keep them moving!
Move them to the right place at the right time!
*Adventure—not Predicament!*
Said that Trio three times.

Let's advent! said I.
And we formed a gleeclub ring around the rooster.

Then they tossed my questions into the air,
tucked the answers into their bosoms,
and said they would start full-time tomorrow.

I'll be there to wake you, said Fay Morgan.
I'm your non-stop stewardess, said Kitty Hawk.
I'll welcome you home, said Ruby Hill.
And away they skipped, as sudden as they came.

Well, if I'm not a changed man, I soon will be
with three new roommates for my single bed.
No more stray feathers! I've met my own flock.
I can stay in one place moving everything around.

So if you need a good muse on your own predicament
go sit in your chicken yard and see what comes out.

## THE GUIDE TO THE MYSTIFYING MOUNTAIN

When in the middle of my life
the dark wood had gone astray in me
and I found myself lying in a snowy despond
on a bundle of middle-aged straw,
at the Feast of Epiphany just before noon
a familiar stranger crawled into my coop
incompletely disguised as a shepherd.

I'm Brother Robert from the lost hills of home,
        he said as he lit a few fires,
Roberto il diavolo is the name I don't go by
though that's how it's scratched on my headstone,
for old Bob's your true uncle and Virgil's his nickname.
And since you have run out of helpful visions
I've been sent on a mission to bring you one
        straight from the High Fidelities.
So up you've got to wake and go for a walk,
we've got to get first beyond this old forest.

Forthwith we set forth, I only half dressed.
No loitering! cried my awesome Guide
and trotted me behind him out of the wood
whence we climbed a mucky mount of humus
up a steep way a mile or two, until abruptly
        Behold! he halted,
This is where you must look.
From here is where you may see it.

But all I beheld were clumps of mist.
Is there some sort of view? I asked.

There most certainly is, said this Fra Diavolo,
and I was ordered to bestow it unadorned
since it's meant for your good rather than mine.
It's a glimpse of your whole life spread out and up
    or at least a half dozen highspots.
It's the Six Components that can make all your ends meet
if you don't try to get around them.
So look! Take a look! Yesterday is already tomorrow.

Look I did, up and down squinting into the mist
till slowly I could make out below where we stood
a giant Wastebasket, bluntly labeled
'Throw away only what you want to keep.'
That, said my Guide, is your First Component
    so make a deposit every day.
What goes out always comes in again.

    Yessir, I said.
By then I had noticed, growing nearer my feet,
an irregular Umbrella Stand, marked
'For going out and opening up'
and a much taller one than my Grandpa's.

Don't worry about being all wet,
remarked my Virgilian friar, unless there's a drought
or you run out of breath on the way up.
That, anyway, was your Second Component
and the Third—in a way—is like unto it.

In front of my arm's length had just sprung open
a Drawer 'For keeping the usual instruments'
especially erasers and pencil sharpeners

plus some fallen leaves from a diary bush
    and a can of Instant Glue.
I'm glad it's so roomy, said I.

Those, said old Bob, are half your earthly essentials.
The other half being higher up are
    a tiny bit harder to see.
Try lifting your eyes more aloft.

And there, right over my head,
as though an angel butler had just opened a door,
extended a silver platter holding
my True-Identity Card.
But even on the jump I couldn't reach it,
    couldn't read it,
I wasn't tall enough yet.
What does it say? I begged my emissary.

It's addressed to You from You, he replied,
It says in a hopeful scrawl:
'From I to I, with best wishes'
and most of the facts are included.
While the backside contains a handy arithmetic
    for figuring in any pinch:
'I to carry, I to drop, I to check, and I
    to the nth power.'

I want it, I need it! said I to him,
And what is the face inside?

Without the right mirror, who are we?
    shrugged my cryptic Guide

and pointed higher to my Fifth Component:
an unblanketed double inner-spring Mattress
afloat like an allegorical cloud
with Cupid in woolies leaning elbow against it
    in a very contemplative pose.

Birth and death make the handsomest couple,
said Brer Robert, pointing now above that odd bedstead
    toward nothing that I could see.
You'll have to uplift your tiptoe for this one
else you won't know what life comes down to.

But I do know! I cried, It's The Kiss! And I see it!
It's the Last and my lovely, the high and my Sixth,
the Waker of sleep, the Sleeper of awake,
it's the deep golden Kiss of God!
O how do I get from here to up there?

Are you game to jump over the fire? said he.
How high's the jump? said I.

That question, he answered, is divided in 3:
1) Plunging in, 2) Digging it up, 3) Bringing it back,
although it's the unmentioned 4th part
that usually trips them up.
Here's a helpful codicil, however,
delivered to me from the Old Lion's mouth
which he asked me particular to pass on to you,
and it says:
    O ye of little face,
    unless ye reach the Quadraplissimus
    and pluck the Decamultiplum
    thou canst not square the root

of the inner circle
and so thou shalt wander aimlessly
now and forever
in the Non-no-nothingdom.

Goodness, said I, is that true?

Of course it is! snapped Fra Roberto,
It was written on my wall in indelible longhand.
O this is enough for you in one day,
I've got other fish to fritter. Ta Ta!

Wait! I called after him,
Is all that you've shown me
some sort of hellish temptation?

He grinned as he slid out of sight:
Call me up whenever you need more advice!
and abandoned me there on that mountain
where my feet had sunk so deep in its muck
I could no longer move.

Mudstuck, cold and alone I looked again
for the six magic talismans of my life,
but all had vanished with the mage who unveiled them.
Nothing now emerged from the clumped-around mist,
nothing except
a long wagging string dangling out of a cloud
like the string to some invisible kite,
like the knotted string to my lost boyhood kite.
And feeling my arm tugged upward
I discovered I
held the end of that string in my hand.

## FEATHERS OR LEAD?

Feathers or Lead?
    asked the Devil of Remedies locking the door
    clamped his stethoscope claw to my belly
    and pricked my liver with his beak.
How does it hurt now?
Feathers or Lead?
I warn you, either answer is wrong!
    said this very same Demon of Tender Mercy
    who had come to nurse me in an odorous gown
    when I lay bedsick with my broken soul
    where he would not let go of the wound.
If you don't feel it yet I can come much closer,
I can crawl much farther in!
    and stood up naked with two heads of hair
    and a scalp between his legs.

Doctor my Doctor!
Shall I last the night?
    I was on my knees in my own hair shirt.
Where is the gold apple core you promised?
Why did you feed me on ghostly bait?
When I begged the medicinal root of my Fall
you gave me an old umbilical to suck,
gave me my own contamination to swallow,
imbedded the ghost in my guts.

Feathers or Lead?
Feathers or Lead?
    and he rattled his teeth in my pelvis.

Lead lead leaden as the jokes of Hell!
For the curse thumped down inside me where
feathers lack bones to fly them.
O Doctor my Doctor!
    I groveled at his hammer-toed feet.
What you put in, take out take back!
I asked for one slice of the bread of life
I asked for one sip of the healing waters
to father my own grown Son made flesh.
Instead I am child to my gangrene brother
who hangs his skull between your legs
and infects every breath in my blood.
For the love of Man at any price
cut my other out of my bowels!
Or I vomit your bargain back!

The trick is known only to the specialist,
    said the Ministering Devil of Chronic Sores.
There remain advanced stages of your complaint.
A diagnosis of the incorrect self
can lead to fatal complications.
If you mistake despair for desire,
mistake your greed for need
and your sentence of death for a book of love,
I'm always ready to oblige.
It's time for another stronger dose,
you're not sick enough yet by far.
    And he clamped my nose and forced my chin
    with his cold wet rubber paws.
Now you must eat the regurgitated loaf,
now you must drink the excremental wine.
Here is your mother's befouled placenta!
    And he thrust her corpse down my throat.

I choked, I spit, I wrenched my gall,
I broke his needle, kicked his black bag—
and when the maggots inside it cried out
I ripped open my guts with trembling hands
and spilled his own filth upon him.

Feathers or Lead?
the dungheap cackled
and slithered out under the door.

## THE BRIDE FROM THE SEA

Between
the waves of the sea
and the waves of the land
I knelt on the sundown beach
mourning my dragonfly voyages
of old ago,
hungering for the root
of that mountain
where yet I might plant my home,
knelt wet-kneed in the dark sand
beseeching the woeful surf:
O share the tide of my tears!

I scarcely expected an answer.
But a blinding wind from offshore
suddenly slapped my face
and I heard in that wind a strange cry,
a woman's dense voice from the sea:
Rise, rise! Take me up!
I call you hero, I await you!

Take me in, take me! Awake me!
I am yours, I will not resist!

Against the fierce wind I gasped
Who calls me?
and could see no one.

Have you not heard me before?
said the fathomless voice.
Long have I loved and languished.
Have you not felt my touch?

What are you? I shivered,
Where do you come from?

I rise on your tides,
I shower you in mist,
I salten your eyes,
I glisten your whiskers,
I sponge your thighs,
I graze your groin,
I loll in your armpits,
I glow round your temples,
I bead your misgivings,
I wean your sighing,
I lean near, I listen,
I encircle, I am . . .

Who? Tell me who?

Unnamed queen of your water kingdom,
unclaimed bride
of your fearful ocean!

What do you ask of me?

Blaze! Scorch! Light!
For fire I thirst! For your fire!
That I may become
  your devoted stranger—
tell you tales of the deep
and tricks of the waves.
That I may become
  your sly familiar—
sing you the powers of great Poseidon,
dance you the currents of Amphitrite.
That I may be your known
  Lady of Unfearful Motions.
Long have you been mine already.
Therefore rise,
  embrace me and burn me!
Else you can never know my true name
nor ever claim your own life!

Shaking with cold I rose to my feet
and opened my arms to the wind:
  Unknowable Betrothed—
  though I perish of it
    I accept the vow!

Abruptly the wind died away
    and I
stood blinking at the surf
only to see rolling toward me
a towering wave too high to outwit
that crashed over my head

and toppled me with it up the beach
    where I found
myself clutching myself only
soaked to the skin.
Yet why was I burning hot
    baptized in my own sweat
        my whole body throbbing
throbbing with exultant song?

        Then I heard
what the song was singing:
        the shock of my joy
    that on a deserted beach
    between the waves of the sea
    and the waves of the land
I had wed my own grief for all time.

VII

# *Tidings*

*Poems at the Land's Edge*

TO STAN BRAKHAGE
*snow leopard of the Rockies*
*fire brother to the scorpion*

*The wilderness under the sea*
*casts a shadow upon the mountain*

# *Soundings from the Shore*

*Upon the mountain*
*the sea is a view.*
*Down here on the sand*
*I view the mountain.*
*Which is the better view?*

## I ASKED THE SEA
*Conversations at Mendocino*

I asked the Sea how deep things are.

O, said She, that depends upon
how far you want to go.

Well, I have a sea in me, said I,
do you have a me in you?

I'll look, said the Sea,
but that's apt to go rather deep.

And she broke a wave over my foot.

*  *  *

I asked the Sea
how to cope with my life.

Yes, She said, Yes . . .

No no, said I,
I want to know
how to be strong like you.

Yes, She said, Yes . . .
kissing the arms of the cove.

*  *  *

I took a morning glory
down to the Sea at sunrise
and laid it at her feet.
But the day darkened and stormed.

A gift should not be niggardly.
Remember that imperiled mariner
who chopped off his finger
and tossed it overboard?

Tomorrow I must take my heart.

* * *

The world, I said,
chirps a roaratorio
of meaningless questions
and wrong answers.
Isn't there somewhere
a quiet place?

Yes, said the Sea.
In the eye of the hurricane.

* * *

Why are you so restless?
said I to the Sea.

I'm calmer than you, said She.
The wind and the moon
like to toss me about
but myself I do nothing at all.
I accept whatever comes
and everything comes to me.
How do you manage that? said I.

Oh, She replied, I have
rather a good digestion.

* * *

Why are you always going
in and out?
I asked the Sea.
Why don't you just
stay put?

I'm not a puddle
or a bush, She said.
Furthermore
I only go out
in order to come in again.
Nothing goes forward
without first going
back.

* * *

Old Mother Sea, I pray you,
you who absorb and reflect
all the collected ponders,
have I another think coming?

I confess the wrongs of my head.
I repent its thoughtless notions.
Have you a tonic brain wash?
I am ready to mind my change.

O Lady of Another Think Coming,
have you a fresh profundity
to help me launch and pilot
the homeward voyage of my ark?

* * *

Let's talk of my dead,
    the Sea said.

Let's not, said I,
    I'm dry on my dune.

But what of the drowned?
    the Sea boomed.

Their ghosts I know,
    said I on the sand,
as I know my own doom.

    Then, said the Sea,
when I wash up the dead
    will you wade in?

I'll swim, I said.

*   *   *

Wading into the surf
I saw in the oncoming wave
a coal of fire ablaze
like the very eye of the deep.

I plunged and reached out.
When I found my feet again
I clutched in the dripping air
a rose-colored tennis shoe.

Said the Sea in my ears:
Love is the element, flowing
and burning, is the fire
in which you swim.

## THE PRINCESS OF THE WATER LEVEL

The level of water is where the princess
came ashore.

She was neither late nor early. She
had been expected so long
we had given up expecting.

She came, however, on time.

For some time the water level had been
uncertain.
Now it was threatening to sink
rather than overflow.

Therefore nothing was more reassuring than
to see the princess at this time.
On time.

And she was younger than she was older,
and very good with water.

She did nothing special with it.
She gazed at it.
And gradually
it flowed. Gentle but constant.
Gradually it flowed. Pure.

So she was welcome to dwell there,
make new friends
or tell old stories.
Because, in good time, she was
certainly
High Princess of the Water Level.

## TRISTAN AT THE SEASHORE

Apathy and delirium sun themselves on the porch.
All the old dragons loll along the beach.
Such lightning has rather a hazy lurch.

The rabbits are very pink around here, said Tristan.
What twitters the duckling dreams?

Catamount jars wilt away in the sand
for the scalawag sock-maker has long since skipped.
Monkeyshine and mollycoddle walk hand in hand
buying mouse-miracles in every shop.

Sloth and wheedling play ball in the hammock.
All the cold boas curl around the deck.
Not much wind for propping up a rope trick.

These glassblowers have very thin bottlenecks, said Tristan.
What withers all goldfish schemes?

## THE DRY-DOCK STRIPLING

*What are you cutting down, my boy?*
*What are you erasing?*
Off the bilgey bottom, off the petrifying weighs
I am chopping the old ballast that has leaned on my eyes,
and now I know a topmast is where I'll look to sea.

*What are you cutting up, my son?*
*What are you replacing?*
My rages will not stutter now behind the grimy burners
where my shovel-thumbs blistered soothing an old furnace,
for off slid the anchor when I launched my own free.

*What are you cutting loose, my man?*
*What are you disgracing?*
No sticker-in-the-mud will longer barnacle my travel.
Now off is rubbed the rust and the glue from my keel
and scrubbed swim the mermaids round my brand new me.

## THE BEACHED CRUISER

I am
a moony old vessel,
I have
garbled many a hanker.

Now I sit
by the ocean of notions,
I sit
on the dry land of facts.

Although
the winds still blow fevers
I know
what my timbers are made of.

And now that
I've got things cleared up
I can
cheerfully rot in the sun.

## IN THE WIND'S EYE

Wonder of<br>
            windowsill<br>
wind<br>
      to the wandering heart<br>
blowing<br>
         wonder full<br>
                      in full view<br>
a view from an elbow<br>
     of<br>
the folded world<br>
                  unfolding<br>
a view from<br>
this windowed I<br>
       these eyes<br>
                  unfolded on<br>
all the world blown to<br>
                      dancing<br>
in the wind of<br>
                wonder of<br>
the breath-taking view<br>
                      of<br>
Our Breather in Heaven

## GOOD NIGHT, SWEET SUN

1.

Lively they sing, and fervent,
the enraptured daughters of the sunset
who dwell in that western orchard
which Mother Earth gave to Atlas.
When the sky is the color of their apples
lively they sing of death.

2.

At the dying light of dividing line
where day and night meet and part
the melting heart of the stricken King
bleeding from a window in the darkening wall
forgives his murder by the falling dark
where day and night part and meet.

## THE SICK BONE

*Cried the sick bone lying on the beach*
Embrace me, O Sea! Heal me with your lips!
Take me in, take me deep, melt me in your mouth,
dissolve my brittle armor and my dried up heart!
*Cried the sick bone lying on the beach*
O great Devourer, swallow me profoundly,
return me anew to the marrow dung of Time!
I want my second birthright! My immortality!
*Cried the sick bone lying on the beach*

## THE SONG OF SANTIAGO DE COMPOSTELA

I am a star wandering the earth
and shining up from its depths
with only this shell in my hand:
      this fragile orbit
      this creature's castle
      this seed from the sky
formed in the womb of water.

Sieving the mica sands of truth
a long time I have been pilgrim
carrying this shell in my hand:
      this craft of Venus
      coquille of St. Jacques
      this star of the deep
fluted with the rays of the sun.

Long have I been a pilgrim star
and this, all I have, holds all I know:
      this shell in my hand
      from the sea.

## WHAT IS BURNING IN THE DEEP?

What is burning in the deep
far below the floating sail?
What is burning in the waters
down down within the whale?

What is burning in the deep
far below the rolling wave?
What is smoldering in the ashes
of Poseidon's blackened grave?

What is burning in the deep
from Atlantis's farewell?
What is flaming to be harrowed
from the ocean's salty hell?

What is burning in the deep
that churns the breakers with desire?
What new creature, what new city,
what new godhead is afire?

## I HEARD IN THE SHELL

  I heard in the shell
  all the hymns of hell,
I heard all the angels crying,
  I heard the earth
  in pangs of birth
and all the galaxies dying.

  I heard in the shell
  the resounding well
of all humanity's voices,
  I heard every shout
  of laughter and doubt
in the crashing war of choices.

  I heard in the shell
  the throb of each cell
from flower and rock and feather.
  But loudest of all
  rang the quiet call
of Yes and No singing together.

# *Neptune's Anchorite*

A STINSON BEACH JOURNAL

TO JOE & ELIZABETH

*Thanks to the tidal wave*
*my roof is decorated*
*with garlands of seaweed.*

O let go, let it go
let the whole kaboodle go!
All the effortfull attitudes
beatitudes
and higher higher thought!
My baby has been drowned in the bath
before I could throw it out.

No more
theorizing, ponderoozing or opinionazing, please!
No more Either Ors
to rock my shaky boat,
no more Problems of, Questions of, Choices of,
nor high Aesthetical Judgments, please O Lord,
no more, O Lord of Things as They are, O Lord,
no more for me!

Because I have my own particular tree
to tend
and though it may be growing upside down
I'm going to climb to the roots
in my own peculiar way.

* * *

Here I dwell beside
the unstill waters.
The unstill waters run deep in me.

Here I sift the mists
of all my journeys
from lost jungles to unfound fields.

Tail of the mountain
rising at my back
I face the West that becomes the East.

This margin of sand
is now all I have
to stand on, fall upon, or be.

Father of upheavals,
Neptune the redeemer,
in which cavern does my Hero sleep?

Sender of bulls,
O great tide-changer,
help me bust my bronco through the deep!

* * *

Dear Dr. Sea,

Teach me to roar and to lilt.
Teach me to wear down my barriers.
Teach me to float on my fears.

Teach me to yield to the wind.

Teach me to contain what I spill.
Teach me to breathe with the world.

So far I have failed every lesson.
Is the whole course over my head?

Yours respectfully,

* * *

I thought I lived here alone.
But a skunk sleeps under the porch
and a swallow over the doorway,
quail nest behind the woodshed
and rabbits underneath it,
a snake lives under the house,
a salamander under my bed.
The voles, the frogs, the raccoons,
the moths, spiders and bats
are all more at ease here than I.

Adaptable bedfellows, can you teach me
how to be at home wherever I am?

* * *

When the fog lifted
I went out to gather driftwood.
Over my head
a seagull was carrying
a sardine can.

* * *

Let it be.
Let it be me
here by the sea
like the boatman I saw in Bangkok—
who smiles by the sunrise river
as he washes
as he pours over himself
a bucket full of the river,
pours over himself
the river to which daily he offers
his spit, shit, and urine,
the river which he drinks
and launders in—
pours it over himself
smiling as he washes
and then, refreshed, sits down
and starts fishing.

* * *

The day is porridge
and the day is sheen.

The wind is savage
but the sky benign,
the horizon murky
but the mountain firm.

The night is torment
and the night is calm.

* * * *

Next to the scotch tape
and the cough drops
two Tarot packs
lean on the flashlight.

What can his name be—
the unknown savior
whose knock I wait for?

Who says he exists?

* * *

I am closer to the sun
than to anything it shines on,
I am closer to the ocean
than to a single wave,
I am closer to the forest
than to any of its pines,
I am closer to a ship afloat
than to any home I have.

I am closer to Arcturus
than to my reading lamp,
closer to a dream of Spain
than to Christmas with the folks,
I am closer to Infinity
than to any grain of sand,
closer to my seven-league boots
than to my woolen socks.

So when my Lady True arrives
to correct my normal focus,
will I recognize and welcome her
if she has no telescope?

* * *

She will not stay for slipping
    slippery away—
my lady of the tidepools
    dripping time away.
I cannot hold her. Gone she goes
    again again away!

* * *

Do you know Ann Seaforth and Dan Fireball,
my unshrinking neighbors who met in a sunbath?

Ann knows the answer. She has given up questions.
Dan grows the lemon tree. And races the dog.

O lemon! O dog! With answers to burn!
O Ann Seaforth and Dan Fireball!

* * *

Ahoy, Umpire of the moontide races!
When may I shoot my thistles at the sun?

* * *

Come on, swab out this shore!
Drain the clogged fathoms,
vacuum the findrinny corners,
sweep everything out to the ebb!

The flood should return improved
by a clearer look.
And he who can float on the waters
may order a glass bottom boat.

* * *

I was lying on the beach
reading Moby Dick
when a dragon fly flew up.

I'm ready, said he.
Are you?

Wait a minute, I said,
till I finish this chapter.

Ta ta! said the dragon fly
and headed out to sea.

*   *   *

Some serpents wiggle more than others
and if you notice any lions loose
let me know if their roar is working
authentically.
The way the frogpond sounds tonight
someone will croak for good before morning.
And where did the canary go
when I put it down the toilet?

Despite the lack of roads around here
one ought to go farther in this world.
The old trails tend to be trappy,
not all the bushes have been burned
and many a lake overflows
at the least expect,
making more mud on the path than
organizers care to foretell.

However, this penetrating Cold
comes direct from Hell, thank goodness!
What a relief after so many false heats!
Keep that vent open! Keep that blast lit!

* * *

O Delivering Angel behind my sickbed,
pull me through the hole in the wall
against which my head is beating!

Let me emerge on the other side
into my authentic shape and name
that my demons no more shall know me!

O Angel of Life, let the death begin!
Return me to my original form
that I have never yet been!

That I may fly with the gods
that I may crawl with the worms
that I may be merely human....

* * *

TRY to imagine
      (I say) TRY to
hold the Bright Brave
            Principle high
Believe in (I say) TRY TO
believe the Promise of
      Light

worn as garment
born from the night
TRY    to imagine it
   (I say)
            TRY TO
(tongue-tied in the dark)

*    *    *

Louder than the surf
is the pounding of
my heart
breaking into sand:
this splintering
clock in my chest
without number
celerity or face,
only alarm ringing
ringing . . .

*    *    *

The house quaked in the gale
and when the door blew open
an Angel was standing there
tall and silvery black,
an Angel with a fishing net.
May I come in? he said.

Trembling into my toes,
Have some coffee, I replied,
What may I do for you?

On the contrary, he announced,
it's what I must do for you.

I am known as Nick of Time
and I have been sent to your rescue.
So hand over everything at once!
Give me every last thing you own!

There's nothing left, I said,
I have thrown it all in the sea.
Is it my life you want?

No excuses! the Angel answered.
You have not surrendered your hopes.
You have not surrendered your art.

* * *

Are you ready, said the North,
to cross the Great Waters?

Are you ready, said the West,
to sink with the Sun?

Are you ready, said the South,
for the journey going nowhere?

Are you ready, said the East,
to try again?

* * *

Okay, King of the undertow rodeo,
lift your trident, let's go!
Send in the roaring bulls,
unleash the foaming horses,
round up the whole seething corral!

Hanging by my heels in midair
I may not be your steadiest rider,
but I'll grab the rigging for dear life.
No one falls anywhere but down.

*    *    *

I recognized it with a cry:
       there
regurgitated by tidewash
stepped on by gulls and picnickers
abandoned how many years
to night, rain, noon
              lay
(lump of dried blood
among wet twigs)
                     the stone!

I knelt, clutching tasting rubbing:
       O stone, my stone,
       lapis of my life
       at last discovered,
       egg of my enduring
       at last returned,
       magical stone
       above all stones,
       miserable stone
       no more than a stone,
       kernel, talisman, nugget,
       O stone, recognize *me*!
       Let me embrace
       the philosopher in you!
       Let you fecundate
       philosophy in me!

From your seed alive in mine
can that tree sprout,
can flower my own
saxifrage incarnadine.

*  *  *

The night lies vanquished by the sun,
I romp in homage to the blaze.
Aswim in the exorcizing light
I douse the moon in a golden cage.

The world lies ravished by the sun.
I rollick upon lucidity.
My skin exhilarantly sheds.
Is that my crutch washing out to sea?

# *The Water Circle*

AN HOMAGE TO LAO-TZU

FOR JAMES SCHEVILL & JOEL ANDREWS

*This poem is set to the music*
*of a Gigue by Corelli from*
*his Concerto Grosso No. 9 in A.*

1.

Down and up they go
the waters that always flow
the rivers that open their veins to the sea
and then return as snow.

Down from arterial hills
their circulation spills
the heart of the lake refills
and down in the valley the river will sing
as it refreshes everything
high or low
fast or slow
from head to toe
scenery
machinery
and makes the poppy grow.
It wakens a sleeping tree
it sets the salmon free
and then flows down
and down
through field and town
to drown in a briny shroud
and resurrect into a cloud.

2.

From brook to hurricane
the changing waters remain
they freeze and flood and evaporate
and then return in rain.

The generous torrent pours
green gifts on all outdoors
uplifts the reservoirs
and out of the faucet the river will run
as it refreshes everyone
high and low
friend or foe
from head to toe
swashing in
or washing out
and makes the baby grow.

It lubricates the blood
it moves the human mud
and then descends
and ends
inside the tide
to lay in the ocean's hand
the sacrifices of the land.

3.

O there's a time when streams run dry
and every road blankets in dust
when ponds are parched with alkali
leaving the trout nonplussed
when there's an oven in the sky
that blackens the meadow's crust

and when in drought
the only wet
is tear or sweat
and old souvenirs of rust.

But down again they'll flow
the waters that come and go
the rivers that bubble their bounty away
and send it back in snow.

Leaping from mountain heights
the juice of heaven unites
all living appetites
and down in the valley it gurgles along
liquidating right and wrong
high and low
and status quo
from head to toe
reveling
in leveling
and making apples grow.

Up and down
it comes and goes
and dies in the bed of the sea.
Up it snows
and down it flows
and so it shall always be.

VIII

# *Gods and Little Fishes*

TO ALAN WATTS

*Far far off is*
*the What too far*
*and near is*
*the Why too near.*
*There goes the Once*
*that went to Where*
*and here comes the Now*
*that's Here.*

# *A Few Profundities*

## PAPA HAD A BIRD
*(A Creation Myth)*

In the beginning was the Bird.
And the Bird was with Big Papa.
And they lived alone at the top of the sky
where Big Papa spent all his time making stars
and pitching them out the window.

Listen, Dad, said the Bird one day,
you ought to get out more often.
This astronomy project is mighty important,
but don't you ever get bored or lonesome?

Listen, Bird, said Big Papa,
I'm a poet and I'm working for posterity.
After a hard day creating I'm perfectly content
to curl up with a new space fiction.

Well, the Bird was bored. He wanted a holiday.
So he packed a lunch from the larder—
a piece of Sunday roast, a jug of Moonshine,
and quite a bit of Divinity fudge—
and he sneaked out the backdoor.

There was no direction to go but down,
so down he flew, until he came to
the old Lake of Chaos—

where he saw, lying on the warm banks,
a serious Virgin mermaid
named Mary Baker Pangloss.

Bird hailed her gracefully
and she sat up amazed.
She had great respect for anything over her head,
and she'd never seen such a Bird before.

In fact, Mary had never seen much of anything.
She told the Bird how hungry she was for a fuller life.

Have you an appetite for higher things? said Bird.
And he offered her his picnic lunch.

Mary was thrilled to have something heavenly
to sink her teeth into.
O, it was divine!
But very filling.
It gave her a tummy ache.
Indeed she didn't feel well for months after.
Because she began to swell.
She swelled up until she thought she would burst.
And then suddenly she did!

And out came—an Egg!
The lumpy pockmarked Egg of the World!

Isn't it pretty? said Mary Baker Pangloss.
It's surely the best of all possible eggs.
And what's more—it's mine!

When Big Papa heard about the whole affair
he was absolutely furious.
He said: That little bastard
is going to cause me a lot of trouble!

## WHAT HOLDS THE UNIVERSE TOGETHER

Everything is stuck together
everything sticks and sticks together
   and we stick to it
   and we're stuck in it
we're part of the sticky too.

Everything is stuck together
everything sticks in the muck together
   and we're thick in it
   we're mucked up in it
we're stuck with Original Glue.

Everything is stuck together
everything sticks in a gooey structure
   and we're stuck to it
   and we're stuck with it
we're all in God's structured goo.

## THE BIRD FROM PARADISE

There is not enough love in this world,
said the Bird from Paradise.

Blind bargains won't feather a nest,
replied the Expedient Hawk,
as a credit risk love is unsound.

Do you honor the earth your mother?
said the Bird from Paradise.

We have quite enough trouble already,
replied the Mechanical Hen,
just keeping our heads to the ground.

Do you embrace the heart of your brother?
said the Bird from Paradise.

What with so much talk after dark,
replied the Graduate Owl,
love is only a useful old word.

Do you exalt the god in each other?
said the Bird from Paradise.

This world is devoted to scorn,
replied the Castaway Dove.
Are things different in Paradise?

There is not enough love, said the Bird.

## THE MAN WHO JUST SAT

Why are you sitting there on the cliff,
you ridiculous man with a grin?
Why aren't you somewhere you ought to be?
Why aren't you laboring gainfully?
Why are you out and not in?

*I'm just sitting here, thank you, to sit, kind sir.*
*It's such a beautiful day.*

Why are you sitting there watching the sea,
you diffident man on a stone?
Why don't you fight for some common good?
Why don't you do what we think you should?
Why are you smiling alone?

*I'm just sitting in order to sit, kind sir.*
*It keeps me from going astray.*

Why do you sit there all afternoon,
you ominous man with no hat?
Are you sick or unhappy or out of your mind?
Are you plotting some plot against mankind?
Why must you sit there like that?

*I'm just sitting here wishing a wish, kind sir.*
*I wish you'd go jump in the bay.*

## THE LIFE OF THE SERIOUS POET

Listen to me, said the Old Man on the sideline,
let me tell you all I don't know.
    O no, said the Poet, I'm busy.

Very likely, said the Woman at the clothesline,
unborn saints are apt to remain so.
    Ho, said the Poet, you're dizzy.

Tell me where, said the Child in dirty tears,
do puppy dogs go when they grow up?
    Run along, said the Poet, and shut up.

Listen here, said the Sea. Look at me, said the Tree.
We both know a lot we won't reveal.
    Dry up, said the Poet, or I quit.

Beep beep, said the Bird, what words can catch me?
Or do you believe I'm not real?
    Good Lord, said the Poet, that does it!

        And so
        he never did much of anything.
        And yet
        we never forgot him.

## THE OPINIONS OF PERSONS

1.

   Jeremy Bing
   said everything
was either Either or Or
   so Jeremy died
   when he couldn't decide
whether life was an Either or Or.

2.

Said that Nasty Old Man on the road
as he set down his unpleasant load:
'Since I now plainly know
there is no place to go
I'll just nastily sit on this road.'

3.

Let the Devil have his lark,
said Old Mrs Nightgown.
Let him peer in the window
or pee in the pantry.
We'll just laugh in the mattress
and let him lurk round.

## MR MOUSE TO HIS LOVE

Come, dear mouse, my housey wife—
keep yourself afoot now
between the hungerers.
As many hawks as doves
        hatch in a treetop—
it's the nature in things.

Running back and forth
blind in our runnels
through the narrow twixt of
        owl and serpent,
through the zigzag middle of
        puss and cheese-snapper
it's a thin but glorious tuck and nip
we have to grow and go in.
But while we run we
are very much among—
        in the very midst of amidst—
all the other blind mice busy on the run.

So nose up now! my Mrs dear Mouse.
Come! Keep your feet afoot for
        the risky go-about and
        long go-between.
We'll never get to Green Cheese Land
mooning in a labyrinth.

## STATE OF AFFAIRS

Every beetle wants to be a gazelle.
If you don't want to notice, then don't look now,
for things are more mixed than they were before.

Why will the hens follow the swineherd,
or the rabbit go ogling all the goats?
There's enough topsy turvy in our barn as 'tis.

Up says the side that's upside
and down says the side that's t'other,
and we've got to keep straight what sides we're on.

But things are even more than a cockeyed mixture.
So don't look now, unless you want to notice
all there really is to see in our mixed-up yard.

## IT WAS THE WORM

It was the Worm who said to me,
Do you seek the ultimate mystery
of where the Inmost Light may dwell?
I'm never asked, but I could tell.

Men search for it in starry places,
in cloistered cells, in pretty faces.
But they go looking with eyelids shut.
I tell you Glory lives in the gut.

Within that dark metamorphic maze
Heaven and Hell conjointly blaze.
What else gives light to Eternity?
the Worm, smiling, said to me.

## I SAW THE OCEAN DRAINING OUT

I saw the ocean draining out
I saw the shoreline dripping
I saw the beach roll out of reach
I saw the horizon slipping
I saw a shark unload an ark
I saw a mermaid walking
I saw a seal turn a paddle wheel
I saw two tuna talking
I saw a whale with a human tail
I saw an octopus giggling
I saw the seaweed going to seed
I saw the cosmos wiggling
I saw the skies had just capsized
I saw the earth had no border
And with all I saw I was glad to see
that nothing was out of order.

## SAID THE ANT TO THE SEA

You're much bigger than me,
said the Ant to the Sea,
and I will drown
in your watery gown
unless I walk carefully.

Ant, listen to me!
replied the Sea,
Though your path looks small
would you walk there at all
if it weren't for me?

Metaphysically that's true,
said the Ant to the Blue,
Then don't forget
when you get me wet
that I also gave birth to you.

## THE BIRDS OF AMERICA

Said the Birds of America:
*quak quek quark quark, hoo hoo*
*rarrp rarrp, gogogogock*
*feebee, cheep cheep, kakakaa*
*coo ahh, choo eee, coo coo!*

And what is the meaning of that?
said the solemn Birdcage Maker.

O nothing at all, said the Old Turkey,
we just enjoy the noise.

Why not do something that makes some sense?
said the serious Birdcage Man.

We do, we do, all there is to do,
said the Eagle, the Lark, and the others:
We eat and sleep and move about
and watch what's going on.
We mate and nest and sit and hatch
and watch the young get on.
We hunt and preen and sing and wash,
we take long journeys and local jaunts
or simply sit about and scratch
and watch what's going on.

That's quite pointless! said the Birdcage Man,
You'll never get anywhere that way.

Maybe, said the Magpie. But when this continent began
we birds were the only two-legged creatures
and we're still very much around.

What's more, the Woodpecker added,
everything man knows he learned from us birds
but he's never enjoyed it as much.

The Cagemaker scoffed: What could I learn from you?

  To do, to do, all there is to do,
said the Heron, the Crow and the others:
  To eat and sleep and move about
  and watch what's going on.
  To mate and nest and sit and hatch
  and watch the young get on.
  To hunt and preen and sing and wash,
  to take long journeys and local jaunts
  or simply sit about and scratch
  and watch what's going on.

O that's absurd! said the Birdcage Maker,
Don't you know the real meaning of life?

Of course we do, said the Birds of America:
  *quak quek quark quark, hoo hoo*
  *rarrp rarrp, gogogogock*
  *feebee, cheep cheep, kakakaaa*
  *coo ahh, choo eee, coo coo!*

# *High Kukus*

I have no desire to move about,
said the Tree,
I'm very attached to my roots.

*

I can't wait to be gathered,
said the Rosebud,
I want to belong to a nice bunch.

*

They keep cutting me off,
said the Whisker,
but that will never stop me.

*

You may have had some hard knocks,
said the Pebble,
but I've been kicked around all my life.

*

I don't know where I'm going to end up,
said the Babbling Brook,
but I'm enjoying the ride.

*

There's nothing I like better,
said the Sun,
than throwing some light on the subject.

*

You always think I'm greener elsewhere,
said the Grass.
Well, sometimes I am.

⋆

That's just your opinion,
said the Pterodactyl,
I think I'm gorgeous.

⋆

I'm madly in love with a frog,
said the Goat,
but she has a crazy idea that it won't work out.

⋆

Before swallowing me whole,
said the Panacea,
see if your solution doesn't need shaking up.

⋆

To think of ending my days covered with catsup,
said the Bull,
makes me see red.

⋆

I haven't decided what to tell you,
said the Computer,
but I'm working on it.

⋆

A little bird told me,
said the Eagle,
and then I ate him.

⋆

I like where I'm sitting,
said the Toad,
What else is a toadstool for?

*

I admit it,
said the Rat,
I'm as much of a rat as the next fellow.

*

Sometimes,
said the Telephone,
I can scarcely believe my ears.

*

I may be infecting the whole body,
said the Head,
but they'll never amputate me.

*

Considering how crazy most people are,
said the Chevrolet,
it's a wonder I'm not smashed up every time I go out.

*

I'm hungry,
said the Bulldozer,
I want a hillburger for lunch.

*

I'm born to blush unseen,
said the Violet,
This beer can is sitting on top of me.

*

Wherever you make your home,
said the Louse,
is the center of the world.

⋆

There will be time,
said the Grandfather Clock,
for whatever there will be time for.

⋆

Of course I'm infinite,
said the Grain of Sand,
but what's the rest of this beach doing here?

⋆

I need something to pick me up,
said the Sweet Pea,
I'm dying on the vine.

⋆

I wish these damn angels would get their feet off my head,
said the Pin,
I've got work to do.

⋆

There are some things,
said the Band Aid,
it's better not to have a hand in.

⋆

Get out of here!
said the Mouth to the Foot.
And with that big shoe on too!

⋆

You've got a nice place here,
said the Fly to the Spider.
Is there much upkeep?

*

If you can't see things my way,
said the Sloth to the Gibbon,
we'll never get anywhere.

*

Once in a while,
said the Whale,
one has to come up for air.

*

We may look weird,
said the Platypus to his wife,
but we have each other.

*

I may be ticklish,
said the Rib,
but I'm still holding things together.

*

I don't know what the left is doing,
said the Right Hand,
but it looks fascinating.

*

There might be someone else inside you,
said the Mirror,
beside you.

*

When things get too tight for me,
said the Snake,
I just slip into some skin more comfortable.

*

What a lovely neck!
said the Noose,
Let me give it a nice hug!

*

When you take a load off your mind,
said the Hat to the Head,
where do you put it?

*

If you are tired of standing on your own feet,
said the Baboon,
try sitting on your own bottom.

*

There's practically nothing,
said the Eraser,
that ever comes out perfectly.

*

Why worry about it?
said the Canary,
We can always crack a little seed together.

*

There are two sides to everything,
said the Coin,
John is a saint and John is a toilet.

*

Going around in theological circles,
said the Dove,
God must get very dizzy.

*

I'm just a victim of prejudice,
said the Devil,
It's high time I was integrated.

*

If the elevator isn't working,
said the Pushbutton,
you can always walk down to the basement.

*

Who's well in whose hell,
said the Archangel,
and well off there too?

*

If you get your nose too close,
said the Grindstone,
you won't be able to smell me any more.

*

When your back is against me,
said the Wall,
why not lean on me?

*

Any minute now,
said the Gun,
somebody's going to do it.

*

Don't worry,
said the Caterpillar,
we'll all come out beautifully in the end.

*

Watch me,
said the Night,
wallop the daylights out of Time.

*

I wish I could lie down,
said the Guitar,
I'm just about plonked out.

*

When I gave up trying to understand,
said the Camel's Eye to the Needle,
then I began to get the point.

*

It's quite easy to be enlightened,
said the Lamp,
once you get turned on.

*

Well, here I am!
Said the Baby,
What are you going to do about it?

*

When you get right down to it,
said Alpha to Omega,
where will the whole thing end?

*

# *All About It*

"INTO EVERY LIFE A LITTLE ZEN MUST FALL."

—*Old Saying*

## THIS IS IT

This is It
and I am It
and You are It
and so is That
and He is It
and She is It
and It is It
and That is That.

O It is This
and It is Thus
and It is Them
and It is Us
and It is Now
and here It is
and here We are
so This Is It.

## THOSE OLD ZEN BLUES

*or, After the Seminar*

*It's not because it is.*
*It's not because it isn't.*
*It is because it is*
*because it's not at all.*

In Zen you can't yen for anything
since nothing can be had.
When nothing is real in reality
nothing is good or bad.

There's nothing in heaven, nothing in hell,
and nothing is what I am.
Something is where it always was
but it doesn't give a damn.

*It's not because it is.*
*It is because it isn't.*
*It isn't because it's not.*
*It's not because at all.*

The life I think I ought to live
is just a thought in my head.
I ought to throw my thoughts away
and believe in nothing instead.

There's nothing where I start from
and nothing I comprehend.
Unless I get enlightenment
I'll be nothing in the end.

*It isn't there because it's there.*
*It's there because it isn't.*
*It's where it is because it is*
*and not because it isn't.*

## BUDDHA LAND

*(A Zen Spiritual)*

I hear the happy sound of
one hand clapping
that old hand clapping
that big hand clapping—
I hear the happy sound of
one hand clapping
all the way to Buddha Land.

*Koan Baby, don't you cry, don't you cry!*
*Koan Baby, don't you cry!*

There's a great big emptiness
waiting for everyone
open to everyone
big enough for everyone—
A great big emptiness
waiting for everyone
when you get to Buddha Land.

*Koan Baby, don't you cry, don't you cry!*
*Koan Baby, don't you cry!*

There's a big bodhisattva
dishing out enlightenment
serving up enlightenment
feeding you enlightenment—
A big bodhisattva
dishing out enlightenment
when you get to Buddha Land.

*Koan Baby, don't you cry, don't you cry!*
*Koan Baby, don't you cry!*

## ROUND TABLE

It's all in your head,
the first man said.

It's all in your heart,
said another.

It's all in your stars,
said the man with scars.

It's all in your guts,
said his brother.

It's all in your soul,
said the man who was slow.

It's all in your balls,
said the fast one.

It's all in your things,
said the fellow with rings.

It's in no thing at all,
said the last one.

## HOW SHE GOT WITH IT
*or, Happy Satori to You*
(A Fable)

She was a Cat
who was doing all right
just as She was
with this and that
just being Her
both day and night
the way a She does,

until one year
(on her birthday too)
She heard a big thought
bellow in her ear:
WHAT IS IT, WHY IS IT,
and WHAT DOES IT DO?

The noise kept her awake,
She was losing her sleep.
So She asked an old He
whose nose was sharp—
a Dog with a beard
who played the harp
and whose mind was deep:
What is It, Where is It,
and What should I do?

Said He at once:
You may think the answer
to such a thought
is as simple as singing

a song
but it's not.

For It isn't just Yours
or any other She's.
It's very seldom Theirs
or what They please.
It's not even Its,
you see.

It is how you stayed in
and
It's while you were out.
It is nowhere
anywhere
and everywhere about.

And that is because
if It ever was,
It can only become
what It already
is.

O really! said She,
Don't be so silly!
What is all this to me?

This, said the Dog,
is the cure for the blues.
This is called
Discovering the feet in your shoes.

It's over my head,
said the Cat with a wail.

No It's not! said the Dog
and bit her tail.

Oww! She yowled
and scratched his cheek.
Hooray! He replied,
Have you found what you seek?

She jumped in his lap
and purred in his harp:
The question wasn't anything deep.
The answer has finally hit me!
I was right all along,
It's as simple as a song,
It's the tail of the Dog
that bit me!

And curling up there
inside his beard
She went snugly
back to sleep.

## ZEN CATECHISM

Is This It Here Now?
This Here Now It Is.

Is Now It This Here?
Here It Now Is This.

Is It Here This Now?
Now Is Here This It.

Is This Now It Here?
This Now Here Is It.

## HERE'S TO IT
*(A Metaphysical Drinking Song)*

Here's to that thing
we won't admit!
Here's to the omnipresent
It!
Here's to the It
in which we sit
and stand and walk
and laugh and spit.
It's in every act
that we commit.
It's our inescapable
requisite.

Here's to the It,
our benefit
that makes the world
immediate.
It is the cloth
most finely knit.
It's all of a piece
but composite.
It is the suit with
the perfect fit.
It always includes
its opposite.

It's not the device
of a Jesuit.
It's much older than
Holy Writ.

It's not a mechanical
counterfeit.
It's a metaphysical
hunting kit.
It's infinitely
definite
and definitely
infinite.

And It's always here
so Here's to It!
And all It says is
Submit
          to It!

## THIS IS IT #2

This is It.
This is really It.
This is all there is.
And It's perfect as It is.

There is nowhere to go
but Here.
There is nothing here
but Now.
There is nothing now
but This.

And this is It.
This is really It.
This is all there is.
And It's perfect as It is.

## AFTERWORD: SONG OF SONG

Do you ever hear it?
Do you know
what your voice is
always singing?

Listen!
It sings
(like everything)
as if no song
were ever sung before like
this

It
is the song you have been singing
all your life

PS3503 R759 L6 1971
+A long undressin+Broughton, James
0 00 02 0202106 9
MIDDLEBURY COLLEGE